Table of Contents (TOC)

Part III

Bond Investing

Intro

Have you ever wondered how rich people got their wealth and then kept it growing?

Did they follow a concise business plan?

Did they become wealthy by coincidence, by happenstance?

Was it luck that drove them to success?

Was it the fear of failure, the fear of being totally unknown that pushed them away from the massive amount of common people?

The answer is willpower, determination and the power of controlling fear and thoughts. The power of turning fear into action.

Because "the man is the master of thoughts, the molder of character and the maker and shaper of condition, environment and destiny".

Most many fail not from lack of education or marvelous personal qualities, but from lack of determination and action, from lack of dauntless will.

Usually what we most fear doing is what we most need to do. That phone call, that conversation, whatever the action might be, it is fear of unknown outcomes that prevents us from doing what we need to do.

At that moment, you need to define the worst case and accept it and do what you need to do. No matter the outcome, it is better trying that regretting not doing it.

Keep this in your mind: "What we fear doing most, is usually what most need to do. "

The big challenge of life is that you can have more than you have got because you can become more than you are at this moment. Unless you change what you are now, you will always have what you got.

Success is something you attract, not something you pursue.

Success is the outcome of your actions, of dedication for your dreams.

Success is looking for a good place to stay. You should be that place.

Success is looking for people who want to become more, who know how to direct their potential, their mind and character, even their destructive thoughts to accomplishments.

The idea of becoming successful is based on channelizing your weaknesses and fears to achieve phenomenal things in life.

Instead of going after it, you work on yourself, on personal development.

Personal development means to define your character, develop talent, unlock potential, improve awareness, shape identity, build human capital and smooth the quality of your life, contributing to the realization of your dreams and goals.

Start defining your long range goals, that's your dreams for the next 5, 10 or 20 years, actually for the rest of your life.

You have got to keep dreaming, because if we stop dreaming, we will lose our direction: what we want to be, what we need to do, where we want to go. Without dreams and visions, people perish. We've got to have something to go for, that inspires the heart, the mind, and the soul.

Don't lose the dream of becoming something unique, the dream of love and enterprise, the dream of becoming one day successful.

Dreaming is the way of shaping your desires and keeping them alive until you accomplish them.

Then set short-term goals. That's you goals for tomorrow, this week, this month, the immediate future. They are called confidence builders. Because we set up this short-range goal, work hard for it and accomplish it and then appears that strong feeling, that strong desire to go for your dreams, to keep pursuing until achieving all of them.

There are three categories of goals.

Economic goals are the first category. They reflect your desire to achieve money, income, businesses, profits, production. You need to make sure you have a plan for this category, because they play a major role in everybody's life, this is why you need to set that plan meticulously for tomorrow, for this week, for this month or this year.

The second category is things. You need to make a list of the things you want to get in life, little things or major things, everything is important for you.

The reason, which is part of the fun of having a list, is checking it all at the end of the day: got it, got it...got it...You will get into a habit: the habit of achieving everything you want to. Another important thing is to celebrate when you check off a major thing on your list. Celebrate your achievements. When you reach something, it means that you worked hard to achieve it.

There are two experiences in our life that mark our existence: the pain of losing something important and the joy of winning. When you lose something, you need to keep trying. When you win, you need to celebrate because is your work that brought that outcome into your life.

The third category is personal development goals. That your goals to be stronger, more decisive, be a speaker, be a leader, learn a new language and learn new skills.

That's what attracts good things to your life: the person you become-more skillful.

When you have totally established your goals, when you have a clear path to follow when you have a strong mission to accomplish, then success is only upshot. There is nothing else that can cloud your path when you know what to pursue.

What you pursue is definitely your dream that is shaping every time you take action, whether you open a shop, you create a website, you work in finance, whether you are investing in something you believe is going to bring you profit.

Our dreams are made up of great ideas. Every idea you have can be your way out to success. So next time you have an idea, think about putting it into practice and wait for results.

The sense of achievement

Achievement is not determined by the amount of money and material possessions, but the accomplishing of the goals you have set for yourself. Fulfillment means to do what you like the most, without being constrained by limits. It is about the pursuit of your dreams and happiness, breaking the chains of biases and fears, coziness, and negative emotions.

Achievement is the outcome of many elements: energy, thoughts, hard work, perseverance, time management, ferocious desire, efforts, actions gathered and ripped in over will.

Successful people know themselves because their immense confidence is shining in a chamber full of hundreds of people. This confidence comes from the absolute consciousness of their strengths and their realized weaknesses. If you want to be successful, you have to examine yourself and to mirror with loyalty to your standards, skills, competences, feelings, and shortcomings.

Part I

Chapter 1

Self-consciousness – the motive of your mind

Self-consciousness dictates what we are. But what is consciousness?

Consciousness is one of the most obvious and difficult aspects we can talk over. Consciousness has been described as the state of being awake and aware of what is happening around you, and of having a sense of self. It covers a wide variety of mental phenomena and it is divided in two: the creature consciousness which is representative for the whole organisms and to particular mental states and processes, the state consciousness.

The self-consciousness is a sense and the most demanding one and it might define conscious creatures as those that are not only aware but also aware that they are aware. "Cogito ergo sum" or "I think, therefore I am" is the notion of a French philosopher Rene Descartes who realized and proposed the theory that the plain act of thinking about our existence proves there is someone to do the thinking process and that is our basic state.

Consciousness is the antagonism between the authentic actions that are guided by the core and the untrue behavior that might be constrained by external expectations. Maybe your genuine love is literature and you want to become an excellent writer, but you parents want you to become a lawyer. Maybe a lawyer could be your profession but never your vocation because having a vocation means to love your career unconditionally. To be honest with yourself means to accept and tolerate the dissension between what you really are (your true self) and what others wished for you to become.

Maybe you don't know yet, but you are a multi-dimensional person and there is an obvious contrast between your core and the "you" that others control (surface you). When you are going to investigate these dimensions, you will find firstly the surface, the exterior stratum, that part lightly seen and influenced by others.

This part of you can be easily shaped by external influences such as environment, social groups, even family. Searching more deeply in your dimensions, you will discover the real you, your core. This fragment of you will take life-changing decisions. When you perfectly discover the dissimilarity between your core and your surface, you will become a conscious person.

I am going to present you a memory test and temperament profile. Write down your dimensions:

- your values and beliefs

- mental strengths and weaknesses

- physical abilities

- social character

- emotional needs

On the right, you have to put the core findings, in order to fit your dimensions.

As an example: A) for your values and beliefs --> "I believe in myself because I know that I'm capable of doing outstanding things."

B) for mental strengths and weaknesses --> "I am excellent at mathematics, but I'm deplorable at Statistics. "

C) for physical abilities --> "I'm horrible at playing football, but I'm very good at running."

D) for social character --> "I'm a lonely person."

E) for emotional need --> "I need a lot of affection."

Your temperament is who you are at your core.

Chapter 2

The power of your mind

"The mind is everything. What you think you become. " Buddha

Our mind is capable of evolution. Evolution represents to achieve the stage of comprehensive transparency. Any environment becomes capable of revealing what sometimes seems to be concealed and mantled. Our mind is distilling her vibration to go beyond the hide-bound substrate of individuality.

Personality limits the potential of manifestation dramatically. You can develop your potential ciphered in your genetic code only surpassing the narrow-minded and restricting vision of your individuality. "There is only one corner of the universe you can be certain of improving, and that's your own self. " – Aldous Huxley

Let's not forget the most revealed thing by science: that everything lies in our strength/power. We have within us the resorts that can change our lives. The only thing you have to realize when you reach your pure "you", the real you, is that you are a creature without limits.

"And you? When will you begin that long journey into yourself?"

Chapter 3

Wake up, hero!

"There is something in every one of you that waits and listens for the sound of the genuine in yourself. It is the only true guide you will ever have. And if you cannot hear it, you will all of your life spend your days on the ends of strings that somebody else pulls. "

We all dream and deserve a wonderful life, full of success, happiness, and emotions. We all sight for financial independence and there are moments in our lives when we fail. But let me tell you that you were born to be successful, you only need to activate the will which is at a standstill. You have unexplored talents and abilities that make you unique. The fundamental status represents the unchaining and application of them.

You were born in the speed era and we have a thirst for time. Your craving for time determines you to want to buy time, but soon you realize that you can't buy the immaterial things. You wake up incarcerated in your daily routine. The twilight and the rising seem to be closer than ever before. Aspirations die from lack of time.

You contort your character just to fit in the finite of moments. Those moments are not dictated by your consciousness, but ordinariness. Then the question that crushes your mind is: "What we are?"

We are marvelous creatures. The only real limits towards what we can't be, own or do are those we set out through our thinking. If you ever thought that you were born in chaos, think about the countless opportunities this chaos gives you to accomplish your dreams.

Firstly, your mind will be fulfilled by a fiery desire to overwork the resources you have inside of you. Then the skepticism and the distrust will germinate in your soul. The essential idea is that you don't have to let them come into your mind. Will and ambition are representative for your success.

The principle of success says that you become what you think most of the time. This spiritual and mental conviction asserts that your extrinsic world is the reflection of your thoughts. Only the will is important now.

The German philosopher Arthur Schopenhauer emphasized in his central and magnificent work "The World as Will and Idea" that the sole essential reality in the universe is the will. Roy F

Baumeister, eminent American social psychology professor said that willpower is "what separates us from the animals. It's the capacity to restrain our impulses, resist temptation – do what's right and good for us, in the long run, not what we want to do right now. It's central, in fact, to civilization".

Chapter 4

Willpower – the greatest human strength

Willpower is one of the most important predictors of success in life. The presence or the lack of it influence whether you are self-confident or not, persevering or not, fail or fulfill your great expectations.

Willpower is a crucial skill when we are talking about achieving goals, taking significant decisions, carrying out tasks. Without willpower, it is very complicated to initiate something or to get to the finish line what you have started.

It is said to belong only to triumphant people, but in reality everyone can mold it. The degree of development depends on your ambition, time devoted to pursuit your dreams, eagerness.

The secret of thriving the level of willpower is to give up to detrimental habits and remodel some of them, in order to increase the power and strength for your goals.

Tips for increasing your willpower

1. **Develop a fair-minded goal and a convenient plan**.

Try to create a S. M. A. R. T. goal, specific, measurable, attainable, realistic and time-based. This provides you a wider definition that will help you in developing your personal and business life because "many people fail in life, not for lack of ability or brains or even courage, but simply because they have never organized their energies around a goal. "

2. Create a list of reasons why it is essential to you to reach your goal, and read this list (even when you don't feel like it) every morning and whenever when you're tempted to give up to your plan.

3. **Trust yourself** whenever you engage in behaviors projected to help you reach your goal or avoid behaviors that would steer you away from your goal.

4. **Set up a plan to be liable for you.**

5. **Respond to sabotaging thinking.**

6. **Identify problems or obstacles in advance.**

7. **Prepare your mind for feeling of demotivation, disappointment, discouragement.** There will be moments when you will be defeated by obstacles, but you have to find the strength to rise up.

8. Reward yourself when you achieve sub-goals. It's very important to keep yourself motivated to do things in order to accomplish your goal.

9. **Focus on the experiences you find "worth it. "**

10. **Get back to the first step when you acquire your purpose.**

Following these tips you will boost your willpower and more, achieve your life target.

But, firstly, you have to wake up the hero who is sleeping inside. Let him out! Give him the chance to shine! He could reveal the genuine size of your being.

One thing I am completely sure about: in the moment when you will be completely conscious of the power within, you will become the master of your destiny, crossing the distance from "impossible" to "possible".

Chapter 5

Perseverance reveals our potential

Perseverance is the most significant ingredient of success in different fields. You can be talented and intelligent but if you give up when everything is against you, you're not going to be successful.

Giving up means to accept defeat.

Abnegation leads to complete overthrow of your individuality. If the approach of the problem is not working, try to find another way, method. If this new method is not working, find another one. There is always a way out for your problems. "Don't quit. Success is 90% perseverance". The meaning of perseverance is to remain steady to a goal, in spite of impediments. Persistence almost always leads to success. No matter what domain your goals have to do with, but if you persevere, you will succeed.

Besides an essential trait, perseverance is also a personal value because it outlines and strengthens your temper which gives you the power to focus on your aims. You have to realize that without strenuous work and determination you can't be successful. After this, you will be on your path to learning how you can use perseverance to accomplish your dreams.

Your level of confidence is vital for your advance and your perseverance. Being doubtful about your competences or overconfident can influence drastically the level of success you achieve. You may not achieve it in the time you envision, but that's just what it means to persevere – keep pushing, keep trying, and don't succumb to frustration and despair until you hit your goal.

Chapter 6

Never speak like a loser!

Do you know how to develop your ability to not give up?

First of all, never speak like a loser, because in this way you will give rise to resignation and defeat. Start speaking words like "hope", "confidence", "faith", "success" and you will start to believe and behave using this new image of you, the image of what you actually are, a great character, a resourceful person.

Negative thinking may destroy your life because you are training your subconscious mind to create a negative life, even if you think those perceptions you have are realistic. In fact, all you have done was to embrace the preconceived idea to see the glass full empty instead of looking at the full half of it. I'm going to present you the pitches on how you can change the way you think and act, in order to get rid of these negative thoughts that have a remarkable impact on your mind.

Track your thoughts

In the daytime, take a break and ask yourself what are you thinking and if these thoughts are negative or positive. Try to note them in a notebook, in order to work on them. You have to keep in your mind the following question: "Are these thoughts effective in order to achieve what I want from my life?". If the answer is "No" you have to change them by supper siding them with positive ideas. Keep digging into your mind until you find those gratifying moments that fill you with positivism.

Repeat this process daily

It will take some time until you will delete this model of thinking. The more often you do this, the easier it becomes. The moment when you will completely erase that pattern from your mind you will start to notice long-term changes.

You attract what you think most of the time

You have probably heard about that scientific concept unraveled in 391 BC by the philosopher and mathematician Platon, the laws of attraction, a concept based on the attractive and repulsive force (what you think or believe is what you will see mirrored in your existence). Changing this aspects and beliefs of your life can dramatically shift your life. But, even if it may seem to be an unchallenging task, it is more strenuous than you ever imagined.

You can apply the laws of attraction and you can get them to work for you, but you need to focus all your energy on this process. Certainly you know that you are made of energy and you attract what coincide with your energy. If you have negative energy, you'll attract negative people and situations, but if you combat that embittered energy, you will magnetize only positive things and people.

The solution for your success stands in the way you are managing your thoughts. Change the manner you think and this will be the first movement in your successful life. Focus on finding solutions to your problems instead of finding excuses and in the end failing. Don't forget that perseverance is one of the most powerful ingredients from the perfume named triumph.

Chapter 7

Introspection – a retrieval process

The principle of introspection is fundamental for optimizing the ideology of perseverance. Firstly I going to present the meaning of introspection and then I will tell you how relevant it is for your development. Maybe you think that there is no gateway between success and introspection.

Introspection is a process of reflection and a technique of "caving "your mind for examining your thoughts, memories, and emotions. This research mechanism was developed by Wilhelm Wundt, a German physician, philosopher and professor and today it is known as self-observation.

At the moment when a person is defeated or overwhelmed by fears, problems, ideas or failures, that person needs introspection in order to reveal the inner motive of his collapse/lack of success. That soul needs to realize who and what he is, to assemble the inward forces and pin down the key for his problems.

Remember that the solutions and the answers to your questions are always inside of you, in a corner of your mind, waiting for you to unravel and exploit them. The broad and profound reflection is the way of divulging all those productive responses.

Practice introspection every day. Look within! Scrutinize your desires and thoughts and find out the truth about you. Find out what makes you weak or strong, perseverant or demotivated.

Honestly, I can tell you that I am doing this every day of my life. I learned this exercise from self-motivation training and since them I'm practicing it.

Let me tell you how I managed to do this: take an event of the day, even if it's a crucial one or trivial one. Bring the whole sequence of the event in front of you, in your eyes (try to contemplate like it is happening now). Bring people, actions and gestures in front of you. Try to analyze your behavior towards it. Start discerning how things thoroughly happened. At that moment, your ego is going to fight with you for the truth because he can't accept any fault.

The egoism is the machinery which is bursting into you, fighting with your lucid thinking. You never knew that egoism is the reason of your excuses, no? Well. . . it is acting inside you. It always tells you that you're right in every situation, no matter if you actually not, with the aim of catching you.

Through introspection, you will understand the egocentric nature of your personality and how you can influence it in order to make her show you the truth about you, to advise you and rectify detrimental aspects of your character.

The last step in completing the introspection process is to find and divide the self shadow from your inner self. What is this? Is the separation between you weak, fearful and narrow-minded personality from your rational, full of desires and expectations, competent and refined inner being, who can advance and fulfill smoldering dreams.

There are five questions you should answer in the introspection process:

- What in your personality needs to be inflated so that you can rebuild/change it?
- What is not true in the dialogue with you?
- What are your unexplored strengths?
- What is your most destructive frailty?
- What does success look like?

Try to give veritable answers to these questions and you will be one step closer to your success

Chapter 8

Confidence reveals your strengths

"Men are born to succeed, not fail. " — Henry David Thoreau

"Every achiever I have ever met says, 'My life turned around when I began to believe in me. '" – Robert Schuller

Confidence is the first secret of success! The conviction of mistrust is a murderous feeling. It kills millions of dreams all around the world. Every day, when you stride the somber streets, you notice scattered faces, sorrowful eyes, pathetic people going slowly on their path of broken hopes.

The eloquent sentence for those who fail in life is "I can't do this!", which can influence their mind and the manner of acting in their pursuit of happiness. We depend on trust every day because it is like the dependence of the engine on oil. It can bring arduous results for success and brand image.

Stability is a key ingredient in emotional and professional success and thriving. In order to boost the personal stability, you need to take well-thought-out decisions, to have well-stability is a perpetual struggle. Once you built it, you have to maintain its level. People fail most of the time from being scatterbrained in its maintenance.

I learned that personal instability has so many complex origins. It may supervene from a latent mental illness: bipolar disorder, attention-deficit or borderline personality disorder. It may be the result of a chaotic education, in which the child never learned appropriate life or relational skills. Fortunately, you can solve all these problems by finding the causes of them and working on them.

Stability is the overriding part of the confidence. Managing stability you can manage the level of your confidence and also strengthen it.

People become outstanding creatures at the moment when they understand clearly that they can do considerable things in their life. When they begin to trust realistically and unselfishly in themselves, they build a deep and unwavering faith.

Chapter 9

Confidence without action is worthless

"Action is the foundational key to all success. "-Pablo Piccaso.

When trust is the ace from your sleeve, failures in life stem from one cause: we can't convince ourselves to take action.

Two years ago I was frustrated with my life. I had a bunch of unfulfilled dreams and passions, I knew I'm capable of accomplishing them because trust was on my side, but I had not achieved a fragment of the things that I wanted to reach. There was a missing ingredient for having the dreamed success- movement. Someone told me to put things into action, to wake up my dreams and put them to work for me. That person told me that if I'm not setting my goals, I'm going to keep them in my sleepy mind to no end, for eternity.

He quoted me the Newton's first law of Motion: "A body in motion remains in motion unless it is acted on by an external force. If the body is at rest, it remains at rest".

So I realized that dreams remain only dreams when you are not acting in pursuance of your goals. There is no amount of positive thinking, knowledge, motivation, perseverance, intelligence, talent and connections that can substitute your taking action. Don't wait for the favorable moment for acting, because they will never be as you wish. This is just an excuse generated by the fear of failure and excessive convenience. Something will always feel off, and your subconscious mind will always justify complacency.

"You must beat your subconscious into submission. "

Make a start! Once you started to act, squeezing the vim from your ideas, it will be hard to stop. Right away you will realize that you're spinning in the carousel of contented dreams.

Every time you take action your fear weakens and your confidence grows.

Chapter 10

The master of your life

Every time you hear people talking about their miserable life, wondering why they can't be successful, why they can't achieve what they want. It may sound familiar to you these words: "I am not successful/pleased because of my partner/my parents who did not give me the right start in life; I'm too old to do what I want to do; I do not have the right resources to succeed..."

Maybe you don't know or maybe you don't want to realize that you are the creator of your entire life. The manner you live is the reflection of your actions and thoughts.

What keep us in this comfort zone are excuses. Even if we have ideals to follow, we don't take any action because we are hiding behind them.

The comfort zone is that behavioral gap where you actions and behaviors are suitable with the routine that reduces the stress and risk. That mental security provides you happiness, rock-bottom risks, low level of anxiety.

"Everything is energy and that's all there is to it. Match the frequency of the reality you want and you cannot help but get their reality. This is not philosophy. This is physics". Einstein wrote this law thinking about the tremendous force of the universe- energy. Everything is related to energy, even your thoughts.

If you do not know, there is a device - electroencephalogram that shows how your brain waves change their frequency depending on positive or negative thoughts. Your thoughts have a direct influence on your physical body as well. Depending on your emotions, you take a decision, which leads to a certain result in your life. So don't forget that every outcome in life has as a motive a thought/an idea.

Are you afraid of living your dreams and failures? Do not sabotage your visions about your life just because you are not strong enough to face them! Remember that "the only battle you need to win in this life, is the war against yourself!".

So wake up and start fighting with you for discovering the real you, for enlivening your dreams.

I am going to present the advantages of escaping from the comfort zone:

Increased productivity

Sometimes we feel so worthless just because we don't have deadlines or expectations to keep us busy and to give us that sense of reliance and consideration. The lack of ambition is what keeps us deep-rooted in that mise en scene. Leaving that unhealthy environment, you can find new possibilities of creating your dreams life and simultaneously more sharp-witted ways to work on your plans.

Easier time handling with new and unexpected shifts

You'll have an easier time dealing with new and unexpected changes. Pretending that risks and uncertainties don't exist is wrong. You have to assume them and try to convert them into positive aspects. Think about the amount of knowledge you can amass while facing with problems and how you can change your character, becoming more confident and dauntless and also you will start to minimize the decision's time. Remember that "practice makes perfect".

You'll find it more convenient to push your bounds in the future

Once you started to taste the benefits of stepping out of your comfort zone, it will feel that strong desire to challenge yourself again and again until it becomes an unconditional reflex.

More effortless brainstorm and developed creativity

Searching for new experiences and acquiring new skills, you improve your creativity and the process of brainstorming will be more efficacious, broadening the horizons of your mind.

Chapter 12

Pragmatic ways to find out what represents you the most

Figure out what is your purpose in this world or why are you searching for a life purpose.

Everyone is wondering about their purposes in life, but few of them reach to discover their genuine motivation. But why most of them fail in finishing this process?

The answer is because they don't pursuit completely this trial and they are not straightforward in doing this. Being honest with yourself is the greatest challenge.

Let's start a quiz. Answer to this questions honestly:

Are you satisfied with your life as it is?

Where would you categorize your life at this moment, on a scale of 1 to 10? If your level of contentment is around 8 or above, you are a fortunate/blessed person and you found your way in life successfully. Remember that life if filled with endeavors and failures but after any storm it comes the rainbow and the sunlight.

Remember that beautiful things come in hideous covers. For those of you who rated your level at 7 or below, let's talk about your sense of displeasure because obviously here is the problem. So make an effort to remember the last time when you felt truly fulfilled/self-satisfied (100 percent contented).

Visualize all the things from that gratified remembrance: what was that memory about? I guess a main part of your answers may be related to the level of given responsibilities which was lower than now or worries. Now start to think about your actual worries and how you can weaken them. I know that this is a heavy challenge, but you have to start by downsizing your worries.

I would recommend you to keep track of your worries using a journal for a week or more.

If you discovered them, promise yourself that you are not going to think about one of them for a week. If it continues to come into your mind, eliminate it and do the same with the other ones. It will be hard in the beginning, but by practicing, it will get easier.

In order to get rid of worries and negative aspects/thoughts of your life, try to focus your attention on great/delightful things from your life. This technique is called positive psychology and it is very useful for changing people's attitudes and behaviors and straightening your energy in discovering the meaning of your existence.

After erasing those worries, your mind will be prepared and free for reflecting about your goals in life again.

The last tips: "Be happy and cheerful with the life you created".

Do not forget that the unique recipe of success is:

Success = Information + Motivation + Action

Chapter 13

Increase your positive thinking

It is very hard to change mental habits and giving up negative thoughts is a great challenge, because that groan of resistance keeps pressing you and you can hear that voice of discouragement in your voice, but it can be done using these 3 top tips.

- **Schedule your habit**

It may sound a little bit weird, but when you are trying to integrate a new habit or routine into your actual schedule, it requires time. It is very helpful to set few positive thinking every day. I recommend you schedule 5 minutes in the morning, 5 in the afternoon and 5 in the evening, exercising these thoughts. Make a day-planner.

- **Specify**

Be specific about what kind of positive thinking you want to engage in, in order to manage effectively your time.

- **Share**

Every time you share your intention or goal with someone else, you are more likely to stay committed to accomplishing it.

Chapter 14

Transform any failure into fuel!

"Maybe you have to know darkness before you can appreciate the light."

Every time you fail, welcome failure with joy, because you are one step closer to success. Successful people succeeded in life because they were always practicing and perpetually challenged themselves to achieve better results and expected fail as an inevitable outcome of raising the bar and striding unimpaired fields. They used failure as a fuel to outstretch themselves and gain superior knowledge, exponential growth and skills.

In this society, many of us are afraid of the idea of failing, that we give up before getting started or we never start doing something.

But you can change your conception working hard, with tireless determination and using the enormous energy within us.

I will give you my seven tips to convert your failures into combustible for inflaming your dreams:

- **Expect failure**

Every failure has its lesson that needs to be discovered. They are a fundamental part of moving forward and going after what you want to achieve. The lack of failures is equal to the lack of action or it means that you are not bold enough.

My advice is that you should expect failures and embrace them as a chance to grow, to stretch and discover new opportunities.

- **Are you taking responsibilities?**

Ask yourself every time if you had a great role in the situation you are at that moment. Are you present enough? Are you playing the victim and waiting for others to do your work instead of being the decisive player?

- **Find the lesson of the failure**

In every failure is a significative lesson we should learn in order to succeed, so you have to find the roots of the problem and to apply that knowledge you acquired in a similar situation you will encounter in the future. The fundamental idea is to learn from your mistakes. Find the breakthrough point in the breakage.

- **Add fuel to the flame**

Let your impediment become the driving impetus to your success. Don't give up, try to use failure as a right set of circumstances to thrive. Ambition and will are the key forces in this process. Use that flame which is burning faintly inside you. Give her fuel enough to burn with glorious lights. Let it shove you to the light.

- **Release and receive**

Releasing useless things from our life (such as failure) we can create more space in our mind to invite things that will work. Receiving goodness you will prevail.

- **Get honest feedback and apply it**

If there is someone on your side that you can count on, ask that person for honest feedback. Discover what you could have done better, what qualities that person finds in you, what from your behavior and personality needs an improvement and what areas you may have missed because we all have blind corners and we need someone to underline them. If you discovered new aspects in your personality you can focus on, apply/use them.

- **Once you succeed, keep it up**

When you have accomplished a goal, don't let your mind decay in that state of motionlessness. You have to put more fuel on the flame. Push for a new highest achievement. Hasten your comfort zone, widening your vision and daring more that you got. Ignite your passion and drive it to triumph.

Chapter 15

The SHORTCUT TO SUCCESS

I've been telling you about setting goals because every start is based on a goal.

You may not have any idea about investing, this is the reason why you took this book, but I will help you discover the real world of millionaires, the outstanding path to success, accomplishment, and willpower.

Becoming a millionaire takes outstanding risk combined with extraordinary luck and another element of the millionaires' equation may be talent.

Becoming a millionaire requires principally patience and discipline.

There are some simple things that can define a millionaire:

They are frugal, but there are exceptions as usual. They have accumulated their money not by spending the money they earned rather than by earning vastly more than other people.

Millionaires are entrepreneurs. They own their own businesses. They may not derive huge income from their business, but their business will become in the future a valuable asset.

Millionaires save. They tend to save more than 40% of their earned income.

Millionaires invest. Their success is the result of investing in an idea. When they follow that idea, when they find out the potential of it, when they get results from following that idea, they don't quit. They don't say: "Ok, I've got some money from it. I can live a simple life spending this money. They are enough for a long time.

When I will finish them, I will see what I can do to get more. "

No, they refuse to think in this manner. They imagine themselves growing their successful idea to its fullest potential. They monetize an idea just to get enough money to continue with it. The value of an idea lies in the using of it.

In the end, they become successful because they do what they like the most. They do what they do because they want success more than they want to breathe. And then, because they follow a meaningful shortcut to success. It is given by implementing the rules of another successful people.

The shortcut to tremendous success:

1.   You need to learn more than to earn.

2.   You need to find a mentor to compress decades of knowledge into a few years.

3.   The key to being successful in adding value and making a difference in the world.

4.   Millionaires have a high sense of purpose, that's why they are more likely to succeed.

5.   Millionaires focus on money the most, that's why they are the ones who have the least.

6.   You need to have your heads right if you want to be successful and it requires educating yourself.

7.   Start your day by focusing on 5 things you are grateful for.

8.   The shortcut to success is the model other people's success; there is no need to reinvent the wheel.

Chapter 16

Eliminate DESTRUCTIONS that stop YOU from reaching your GOALS

In order to achieve goals, you need to change your behavior. If you want to become a millionaire, you need to follow the millionaires' habits and eventually become a better version of that prototype.

Because right now you are not ready to make a start, because you haven't developed the needed habits, you haven't eliminated the unhealthy and unproductive activities and the distractions, you can hardly figure out what is the best way to follow.

You need firstly to prepare yourself for success. Achieving what you want is absolutely possible. You just need to fall in love with consistency and start taking a step each day towards reaching your goals.

Remember that I told you that you need to set goals.

But before taking action, before making them become real, you need to eliminate the things that not only slacken your progress but also keep you away from moving forward.

The first factor is perfectionism. Perfectionism is infectious. So many people have strong desires within themselves and truly want to achieve their life goals. But they are greedy and unappreciative even before achieving what they want, and dream of reaching more than they deserve. Some of us want to see amazing results without acting. They want it now because they think they really deserve it.

This is one of the wrong things that people do in their lives.

You need to be happy and grateful for what you have, no matter how little that is, because there are people, on this Earth, that have much less and still find the reason to thank for it.

When you are grateful, you reach abundance. That feeling gives you the power to turn your life into something more. You will feel the fierce desire to work for it and enjoy the outcome of your labor.

The second one is failure, because we tend to see failure as an end of our trials. Most of us fear it and don't even try to do something because they fear of not succeeding. That's why, most of the time, people don't see their dreams becoming a reality. They are too far from achieving them, they get stuck before trying. It seems that fear is more powerful than their desire to achieve dreams.

Jeff Bezos, the founder and CEO of Amazon. com said that: "I knew that if I failed I wouldn't regret that, but I knew the one thing I might regret is not trying. "

We are more afraid of failure than we are of inaction. What we don't know is that failure contains within it the chance of success. It is a predecessor of it. If we try and fail, we know what we did wrong. Next time, we will know what to do better. In every trial is a small chance to succeed and a small chance to fail. But how to know the result if we don't even try?!

The failure is the proof that you're trying to change something in your life, that you are doing something in your life and you're not giving up.

The third factor is focusing on the end results.

Every great result is based on small steps, gathered for a single cause. Everyone is eager to get the results of their labor. There is a strong feeling of impatience that makes us want that outcome right now, at this moment.

We need to realize that things don't work this way and we need to enjoy the entire process, step by step, before reaching the faultless end.

The fourth one is taking big steps.

When we set goals, we establish a certain path we need to walk before getting what we want. The purpose of it is to make us stronger enough to handle the success that's waiting for us.

That path is made of many steps- small steps because they are those that can defeat the fear of trying. The big steps make us worry, fear or not even try.

Next time when you set goals, divide those goals into small steps until you get a list of simple tasks to do each day. The success of this kind of list stands in its power to influence your confidence once you have finished every task for a day. It will be impossible to say no to simple tasks that bring you the joy of winning.

The fifth factor is finding excuses for not doing something.

There are so many excuses you can say to yourself just to not feel guilty about your inaction.

You may hear yourself saying: "I'm not ready", "I don't have enough time/money/experience", "I'm too old/young", "It will take too long", "People will laugh at me". "Most people don't succeed anyway, neither will I."

In reality, you mind is so tricky and prefers to stay in that comfort zone, because when you do the same old activities and tasks on autopilot, there nothing new that can occur. There is no failure when you go on the same path every day. There is no chance for something wrong to happen.

The fear of failing is more powerful in your mind than the power of taking action, That's why it's making up all these excuses, that can often sound so convincing.

You need to erase all these excuses. It may sound very ridiculous to hear them again after you have eliminated them from your mind. If you choose to keep them, your life will never be different because you can't embrace change.

Changing the pattern makes you realize the enormous possibilities you have to make things become a reality.

The sixth factor is called procrastination.

It is one of the factors that stop us from taking action towards our goals, so we need to stop it.

Now is the perfect time to do what you want. If you decide to take action any other time, it will be too late.

Taking action now means to work for shaping your successful future, to create your future.

Procrastination keeps you away from working on what you believe it, keeps you away from productivity.

The cure for procrastination is action. Acting immediately, without thinking and giving your mind time to come up with excuses is the most powerful solution.

Stop doubting your abilities and competences. Stop fearing failure. Start molding your future every day and get closer to the final result.

The seventh factor is the presence of expectations.

Expecting too much brings disappointment in your life. There are things you can't control, even if you try to. It is a destructive behavior.

You expect facts to turn out in a certain way, you expect people to behave like you imagine them to, and whenever that doesn't work out, you feel upset and lose motivation to take action.

The solution for disappointment is to stop living in a world created by your complex mind. Stop making scenarios and accept the thing as they are.

The eighth factor is the presence of distractions.

There are people in your life that will tell you that you can't do something, that will make you doubt yourself, your abilities, and the power to make a change. They will make you lose hope if you listen to them.

There will be so many distractions and temptations on your way to success, you may feel overwhelmed by them. You may fall in that carousel of inactivity and feel that life is unfair because others have so much time, can eat whatever they want, can buy what they want, and you can't.

The reality is quite different. You choose when and how much you work on your goals. You choose to strive for a better life while others continue to prefer the easier way of living their life: a life full of temporary happiness.

Setting goals and acting in order to achieve them makes you avoid distractions.

Tony Robbins said that "Setting goals is the first step in turning the invisible into the visible".

The ninth factor is the lack of consistency.

Without continual growth and progress, success and achievement have no meaning.

Progress is neither automatic nor inevitable. Every step toward your goal, every day, brings you more close to defining your success. If you don't work each day, you won't see any progress.

Consistency in the things you do is a trait of successful people. As you make progress, day by day, it becomes a habit.

You can't succeed without consistency.

Chapter 17

THE STARTUP OF YOU

A successful startup is the result of being able to create your dream and turn it into reality.

There is a set of beliefs are any startup founder should have.

Many founders are not aware of their competencies, abilities, and beliefs. But they are so important for the personal life and also for startups.

We don't realize our power of changing the world in which we live because we were handcuffed and strained to believe that we are only labor that creates labor.

As Muhammad Yonus said, "We forgot that we are entrepreneurs." We forgot that the essence of the marvelous things which exist in this life stands in our power to create it.

We need to rediscover our entrepreneurial instincts and use them to recreate a new world, without strings, without being only a resource in the organization. You represent something for a company as long as they can use you to bring benefits for it. You are nothing more for them.

And you were forced to think that your happiness is a stable, full of responsibilities, overwhelming and stressful workplace. This is not happiness. This is not your life. Your life should be the joy of feeling the freedom in every bone, every nerve cell.

Some of us manifest this gene of entrepreneur since childhood when they try to make money from different small trades or "businesses" as selling eggs to old people. Some of them wash cars, take care of dogs or kids just to make some money.

They soon discover things that bring them profit and they decide to continue doing that thing. They expand it, they turn it into a real business. In fact, they discover how to make money using what they love to do. At 21 they have their own business, which is the result of finding what you like to do and succeeding on it.

In one word, they become ENTREPRENEURS. They make a startup in their career.

Most of them don't follow their instinct because they encounter personal barriers that cloud their impetus.

They don't think they are self-sufficient. They can't act on their dream. One of the most paralyzing obstacles that individuals are facing is fear.

It is not the same as being cautious. When you are cautious, you weigh the risks and rewards and make a decision based on your analysis. Fear paralyze and prevents people from chasing success.

They don't make a start because they are quite sure from the beginning that they will fail.

What most of them don't know is that fear is based on false evidence appearing real. It is something that we create. And once it was created, it is tormenting us with excruciating thoughts. Since as it comes within you, only you can stop it.

There will be all the time obstacles that you perceive as barriers to venturing into something new, like changing your career path and exploring whether entrepreneur or business ownerships.

Fear will tell you all the time that now is not the right time for you and you should wait for that moment. If you can defeat it, you will finish waiting for a change that will never come because you don't have the power to make a start.

You will be waiting for someone to convince you, not to tell you: "Now is the right time for you".

But no one cares about you. No one knows how much you desire something and no one will ask you if you need something. The solution is to educate yourself, to master fear and unleash your potential.

Start by considering these strategies to finally achieve your dreams:

Start with why.

What is your "why"? Define the foundation of your new career path, exploring the possibilities and evaluating the options you have to realize your dreams.

Discovering the primary purpose in life will be the driving force. It will become the why behind the what.

You need to identify your strengths and weaknesses, your opportunities, and threats and find out if they lead to skills.

Then, analyze your list with short and long term goals and define them by the benefit they bring income, wealth, lifestyle, equity. What type of income do you need to generate? What kind of wealth and equity would you like to achieve? What kind of lifestyle do you want to reach by pursuing those goals?

When you have the answer to these questions, you discover what you should change, you know what kind of person you want to become in order to acquire what you most dream of.

Say "Hi" to unknown and keep an open mind.

The most successful people in this world are not those who have followed the field they have studied at university. They have discovered that you can't always do what you know to do, what you love or enjoy doing because it doesn't guarantee success.

They figured out that they don't necessarily need to be in love with something to capitalize on. You just need to adapt your mind and your behavior with the market demand and find out possibilities to make money.

Maybe you are not trained in that domain, but you will definitely learn it if you want to create wealth on it. Maybe you will love it after practicing and achieving results. The idea is that you have to be open-minded for facing thoroughgoing and radical changes in life.

When talking about embracing the unknown, you have to adapt your character to different situations and conquer the fear of unknown. Every start is faded by this fear, but you have to look at the bright side.

Every start has something magic in its essence. Every day is a new opportunity. You can build success or you can embrace failure. At the end of the day, you are responsible for your success and your failure. Make that start as soon as possible and don't abandon it. Don't be afraid of failure. You were born to fail and start over again and again until succeeding.

Start a business on you own. Assume your acts. Start looking at that business as a vehicle to attain the way, the income, lifestyle, wealth, equity goals.

Don't forget that being afraid of unknown means to stifle the potential future success and lead you down the destructive path.

Start seeking a safe haven.

The fundamental step toward success is creating a solid foundation. It means to evaluate your opportunities and options instead of thinking about limiting fears. Then start acting.

There will be obstacles in your new life adventure. But you should explore the potential of your idea and overcome any obstacle, persevering through anything that comes your way.

PART II

Chapter 1: Understanding the impact of Financial Globalization

Facing challenges

The world of finance can be extremely intimidating, but I strongly believe that once you have gained the knowledge, the major concepts, once you have understood that you need to resist to failures and breakdowns, there is nothing else to stop you becoming rich.

This great financial world can offer you huge possibilities to develop yourself and reach the supreme level.

But the major issue of our time is the sustainable development of this world on three levels – economic, social and environmental, because we need to face enormous challenges and evaluate our progress at the end of the line.

Nowadays, more than 1 billion people are still living in extreme poverty, and income inequity within and among many countries has been rising. The production patterns and the unsustainable consumption leaded to high economic and social costs while most of the people struggle to live on the edge of subsistence.

There are many reasons why the world has got this turn: the impact of change in different work fields, the income inequality, the poor importance given to the long-term financing -investments, the changing of demographic profiles, economic and social dynamics and the advancement of technology and trends than drove to the deterioration of the old environmental system of the organization, where people used to play a fundamental role in achieving the purpose of the company and also promoting and making visible the vision of it.

If we analyze the change in technology, we can see marvelous benefits but also it has its disadvantage: not all of our employees can assimilate the new change, can learn fast and continue to work in the most productive manner. They need time to face the challenge of the new era, the era of technology.

But those who succeed in life are those who really want to take charge of their life and personal development. They succeed because they know that nothing is impossible and their purpose is far beyond any limit.

They learned how to make money from their job or being their own boss. They have found different ways to capitalize on.

What I'm going to present you from now on is the world of investing. It may be challenging and risky, but you will definitely become one of those millionaires who love being their own bosses and spend every moment in their own way, as they have dreamed to.

Investing is the smartest way to secure your financial future and begin letting your money make more money for you.

Don't think about an investment as a way to you leave your money alone and wait for success, because success is not guaranteed in this way.

You need to know three things in order to become a successful investor and make sound investing decisions:

1.   **Knowledge**, because it empowers people. It makes them stronger.

A basic background about investing should be the first step in your investing career. Developing an understanding of basic money management does not require becoming an expert on all aspects of investing. You don't need to dedicate years of your life to studying every aspect of corporate finance before buying a stock or investing in dividends.

2.   **Training**, because practice makes things perfect and there is no difference when it comes to mastering your investments.

Maybe you are wondering how you are supposed to practice investing without losing actual money...The solution is very simple: try an online free stock market simulator. You can get a mock account with faux-money and can buy and sell all day, feeling the sense of risk without losing real money and with no real risk.

3. **Experience**, because there is no substitute for studying in the "school of experience".

At some point, after learning and understanding the mechanism of investing, you will start practicing real investing and gain real experience.

Investing can be scary. It is just because in our genetic code is printed the fear of losing, which is much stronger than the one of winning something.

The fear of losing has such a significant impact in our decisions, that it is called loss aversion. The fear of losing makes people take poor choices, makes them go for the least-chance-of-defeat decision, which is not a wise strategy and it won't turn you into a winner.

People tend to think that a risk (one of investing money) is worth taking if there is a sizeable benefit of it.

This way of thinking holds people back from achieving their full potential. They can reach the ultimate level of development because they avoid taking any risks.

It seems that "fear motivates people about twice as much as greed does".

If you truly want to garner investments experience, try leveraging someone else's experience. Seek experts and follow their advice.

Chapter 2

Understanding different investment vehicles

Discovering the value of stocks for your portofolio

The simple definition of a stock could be that a stock is the share in the ownership of a business, a publicly-held company. The stock itself is a claim on what the company owns- assets and profits. When an investor decides to buy stocks in a company, he becomes part-owner.

If the company goes well, experiencing an increase in profits or commercial venue, which is the ability of the company to attract customers for their products or services due to their position on the top of the market or due to the quality of their products or services, the value of the stock will probably go up and the company will pay a dividend- a reward for the investment.

If the company does poorly, the stock will probably lose value.

The amazing thing about stocks is that their value comes from public perception of its worth. It means that the price of a stock is driven by what people think it is worth, not from what is actually worth.

Their price is influenced by customers/investors. When they want to buy more than to sell stocks, their price goes up. Their price goes down when more people want to sell than buy stocks.

Get acquainted with bonds

A bond is a debt investment in which an investor loans money to an organization or corporation which borrows the funds for a defined period of time at a variable fixed interest rate.

Bonds are used to raise money and finance a variety of projects and activities by companies, municipalities, states and sovereign governments.

The owner of the bond is called debt holder or creditor of the issuer.

The interest of the bond is the purpose of the investment.

The term of the bond can range from months to years, at the end of which the issuer pays back the value of the bond in full.

Any investor should be interested in an investment on bonds for a long-term because the longer the life of the bond, the higher the interest rate.

There is a short axiom that defines the investment in bonds and you should consider it: the higher the risk, the higher the return.

Understanding the commodities market

When you decide to invest in bonds or stocks, you invest in what they represent. The piece of paper you receive when you invest is worthless, but what they promise is valuable.

A commodity is exactly the opposite of stocks/bonds, it has an inherent value, which is capable of satisfying a need or desire.

They are valuable because people need them for use or for accomplishing a need.

Many investors trade commodities by buying and selling futures. A future is an agreement to buy or sell a commodity at a certain price sometime in past.

The buyer of the future hopes that the price of the commodity will increase in the future. The seller hopes that the price of the commodity will go down, so he can buy the commodity at a low market price and sell it to the buyer at higher-than-market price.

Discovering the high potential of investing in properties

Investing in real estate can be a very profitable asset, but it is not without assuming a substantial risk involving maintenance and market value.

There are lots of different ways that you can invest in properties.

You can buy a home and become a landlord. You pocket the difference between the mortgage and the rent you receive from the tenant.

You can buy a home in need of renovation, fix it up and sell it as quickly as possible.

You can invest in mortgages bundled together as complex securities.

This type of investment is an enormous opportunity on a long time horizon, because the value of real estate is rising in a given time, which is definitely a long time.

Investing in real estate for a short period is not a guaranteed investment.

Chapter 3

The Financial System

The complex relationship between economy and finance reveals the fundamental importance of the economic initiative, which gives rise, for instance, to pecuniary or financial relations, and also to the finance response which determines and keeps the economic actions and initiatives in the limits of minimum social efficiency.

Money, the financial relations' vector, represents the expression of efficiency and quality of the economic activity.

Money is the social validation of the volume and quality of the economic activity, which cannot be manipulated or influenced through the economic agents' actions or approaches, through a mechanism which is similar with stock market.

In the context of the modern economic history, the main objectives of a company were the maximization of the profits and the growth of the company's value.

The stock market is divided into two fundamental parts: the primary market and the secondary market.

The primary market is the place where the new issues are first sold using the public offerings.

Here, most of the shares from investment banks are purchased by institutional investors.

The other part goes to the secondary market, where the participants include both individual and institutional traders/investors.

The manner of trading stocks is called exchange.

The two biggest stock exchanges in United States are the New York Stock Exchange, founded in 1792 and the Nasdaq, which was founded in 1971.

Chapter 4

Mastering the World of Stocks

What is a stock?

Stock is ownership.

The ownership is when you get a piece of every desk, contract and trademark of a company where you have decided to invest. You own a slice of every dollar of profit that comes through that door. The more shares you buy, the bigger the stake becomes.

The intrinsic value of stocks

When they think about the stock exchange, most people picture a scene of frantic activity, with traders in good-looking jackets jostling simultaneously for position, shouting commands, making strange hand signals, writing up orders.

But there is huge work behind this frantic spectacle. There is a methodical and organized system of trading, in which the price of the stock is set genuinely by rule of supply and demand in an auction selling. Shares are sold to the highest bidder from the stock market.

The stock market is a daily referendum on the value of the companies that trade there. The main daily question of the brokers, after taking in the day news and distilling them, remains: Will it help the companies I own make money in the future of will it prevent them from doing so? Because any harmful impact on the company can lead to a fall in the price of the stocks or contrary, a huge turnover or strong economic increase will lead to a high price of stocks.

The supreme measure of value for stocks on the market is earning/profit. Wall Street is obsessed with this value.

Companies need to report their profit four times a year and investors deepen these numbers, expressed in earnings per share, trying to identify and establish the present health and future potential of the company.

The stock valuation is the name given to the financial method of determining the value of the company and their stocks.

The reason of the valuation is to predict future market prices and potential market prices and also for obtaining profit from price movement- when the stocks are undervalued, they are bought and when they are overvalued, they are sold, assuming that undervalued stocks will increase in price while overvalued stocks will fall.

The stock valuation is based on the fundamental financial indicators such as the intrinsec value that refers to the value of a company, stock, currency or product determined through fundamental analysis without considering its market value. It is determined by predictions about the future cash flows and profitability of the company.

There is another method to determine the value of a stock, which is based on the comparison between the supply and demand of stocks on the market.

The first type of valuation highlights the value created by cash flow, sales and fundamental earnings analysis.

The other one is determined by how much an investor is willing to pay for particular a share of stock and how much another investor is willing to sell a stock for.

The market valuation is driven by short-term stock market trends and it becomes very hard to predict the value of the stocks on long-term using it.

There are many different ways to determine the value of stocks, but the appropriate valuation is the result of combining these methods and achieving the most valuable option. Such an analysis about the value of a stock requires gaining knowledge in finance and statistics and the ability to understand them and make effective and real predictions.

Chapter 5

Understanding Valuation Ratios and Fundamentals Data

Earnings per share- ESP

The earning per share is the net income of the common shareholders divided by the number of shares outstanding.

It is one of the main indicators of profitability.

ESP= Net Income-Dividends on Preferred Stock/Average Outstanding Shares

The high-quality ESP means that there is a true representation of the earning of the company.

The best way to evaluate the quality of the ESP is comparing operating cash flow per share with reported ESP.

On long-term run, this method shows the truth about the position of the company.

The company can show a positive earning on the income statement while also bearing a negative cash flow. But for a long term, the company has to borrow money to keep operating. At some point, the bank will stop lending money and ask to be repaid. A negative cash flow then will indicate that there are fundamental operating problems: either the inventory is not selling or receivables are not getting collected.

Cash flow is a rudimental measure for Wall Street. They know that companies that don't generate cash won't resist too long on the stock market.

Price to Earnings (P/E)

The price to earning is determined as Market value per share divided with earning per share (ESP).

If a company is trading at $50 a share and earning over the last 12 months were $2 per share, the P/E ratio for the stock would be 25.

A high P/E highlights that investors are expecting higher earnings growth in the future compared to companies with a lower P/E. To be useful for statistics, the comparison has to be made between companies from the same industry, because each industry has different growth prospects.

Growth rate

The growth rate is the amount of increase that a specific variable has gained within a specific period or context. This represents the compound annualized rate of growth of a company's revenues, earnings, dividends, even macro concepts, such as the economy as a whole.

Growth rate (PR) = (Vpresent-Vpast/Vpast)*100

PR= percent rate

Vpresent=present or future value

Vpast=past or present value

The annual percentage rate is determined by the percent growth divided by N, the number of years.

Price Earnings to Growth (PEG) ratio

This method has become really popular because it is more efficient than price to earnings. There are three factors that are considered: the price, earnings and earnings growth rate.

To compute the PEG ratio, the forward P/E is divided by the expected earnings growth rate. The ratio is expressed as a percentage.

If that percentage overcomes the limit of 100%, the stock becomes more and more overvalued. As the stock falls below 100%, the stock becomes undervalued.

It is believed that P/E ratios should reach the long-term growth rate of a company's earnings.

A suggestive example of how to use PEG ratio to compare stocks:

Stock A is trading at a forward P/E of 16 and expected to grow at 23%.

Stock B is trading at a forward P/E of 30 and expected to grow at 26%.

The PEG ratio of stock A is 16/23=70% and for stock B is 30/26=113%.

According to the PEG ratio, stock A is a better purchase because it has a lower PEG ratio, so you can purchase its future earnings growth for a lower relative price than that of stock B.

Return on Invested Capital (ROIC)

This indicator shows how much money a company makes each year per dollar of invested capital. The invested capital is the amount of money invested by stockholders and debtors in the company for growing/expanding it. The ratio, expressed in percentage, approximates the level of growth that expected.

This ratio underlines the investment return that management is able to get for its capital.

The higher the number, the better the return.

The ratio is obtained by dividing the net income to the invested capital. The invested capital is determined by adding the stockholders equity (the difference between the value of the asset/interest and the cost of the liabilities of something owned), the total short and long term debt and account payable, then subtracting accounts receivable and cash, all these information is taken from the balance sheet.

Return on Asset (ROA)

It is the ability of the company to make money from its assets. It is determined dividing the net income to total assets. It is not the best indicator used to establish the company's potential.

Price to Sales (P/S)

This indicator compares the current stock price to the annual sales. It determines how much the stock costs per dollar of sales earned.

To compute it, take the current stock price and divide it to the annual sales per share. The annual sale per share is calculated by taking the net sales for the last four quarters divided by the fully diluted shares outstanding.

It is not an efficient indicator of the company's potential because it doesn't take in account the debts of the company. If the company is highly financed by debt instead of equity, the sales per share will seem high and the P/S will be lower.

Price/Cash Flow

This ratio is used to compare the company's value with its cash flow.

It is determined by dividing the company's market capitalization (the total dollar market value of the shares outstanding of a publicly traded company) by the company's operating cash-flow in the most recent fiscal year or dividing the per-share stock price by the per-share operating cash flow.

The value of a stock is determined by the value of this ratio.

The lower the stock's price/cash flow ration is, the better value that stock is.

Price/Book value ratio

It is used to compare a stock's market value to its book value (shareholders' equity).

It is calculated by dividing the current closing price of the stock by the latest quarter's book value per share.

P/B ratio= Stock price/Total Assets-Intangible Asset and Liabilities

This ratio provides investors a manner to compare the market value (what they are paying for each share) to a suitable (conservative) measure of the value of the company.

If the company's stock price- market value is lower than the book value, there are two major possibilities to explain it.

The first scenario is that the stock was undervalued unfairly by investors because of some transient circumstances and it constitutes an attractive buying possibility at a bargain price.

This is the perspective of a value investor. They believe that the company fundamentals are still in place and they will lift to a much higher price level.

The second scenario is that the market's low opinion and valuation of the company are correct and in the near future, the stock investment will be perceived at its worst or at its best as being a steady investment. That's the way value investors think in their investing's decision.

There are two indicators that an investor needs to monitor in order to get the right and authentic picture about a particular stock:

The **Short Interest** is the number of shares that investors are currently short on a particular stock.

Short Interest Ratio is the number of days, based on an average trading volume of stock, that it would take all short sellers to stifle their short situations.

There are two different traders on the stock market: those who believe that the stock price is going to go up and those who believe the stock price is going to go down.

Those who think that the stock price for a particular stock is going to fall down will redirect their money elsewhere by investing in other stocks.

If stock traders believe completely that a stock is going to go down, they will sell the stock as soon as possible.

If an investor knows how many shares of a particular stock have been sold short is a suggestive indicator and provides a glimpse into the investor perspective surrounding that stock.

The big picture of a stock can be executed by monitoring the trends of short interest and short-interest ratio numbers.

Some analysts believe that securities with low short interest ratios are less likely to experience price falls and short extortions.

There are some analysts who believe that high short interest are more likely to experience price increases due to the decisions of short sellers to buy the securities to cover their short positions.

The most appropriate way of understanding the profitability of an investment is to analyze multiple valuation ratios and fundamental data.

The Market Valuation

There is a fundamental efficient-market hypothesis based on the assumption that the stock market is a well-organized market, with a large volume of transactions and the market price is determined effectively and economically using relevant information to the evaluation of the stock.

New studies made on the behavior of the stock market show important deviations from the fair price of the stocks.

The fundamental economic criteria is not enough eloquent to determine the real value of the stocks. There is another criteria, based on market that has to be taken into account- market-based valuation.

That indicator is called potential price range and is determined taking into account the market behavior aspects.

Major types of risk for stocks investors

No investment is without risk.

Investing in stocks is a risky business because there are risks you have control over and others that are out of your control and you just need to guard against them.

If an investor wants to build wealth over time, he needs to accept a significant amount of risk.

There are four major types of risks that investors face when they decide to invest in stocks. They are caused by market and economic shifts.

Market Risks

Market risk considers a broader picture of the economy: production, trade, consumption of good and services, investments and savings.

Understanding the market risk is linked directly to mastering the basic economic concepts (output and income, unemployment, inflation and deflation), macroeconomic models (aggregate demand, aggregate supply, IS-LM model, growth model) and policies (monetary, fiscal policies) and having a clear image about the factors that lead to the development of general economy.

Investors have the duty to understand and use these concepts and variables in making predictions about investments and their risk. They have to accept that the overall economic conditions of the country-or even the world- will cause the investments' value to fluctuate.

A market crash or decline could crush the investments' performance, even if the quality of the investment remains the same.

Stocks perform better during a bull market (a market in which share prices are rising, encouraging buying) which happens in economic growth and poorly during a bear market (a market in which the share prices are failing, encouraging selling) in recession.

Inflation Risk

Inflation is a general price increase across the entire economy. The opposite, when prices decrease, is deflation. Economists measure these changes in prices using price indexes. Inflation occurs when the economy becomes superheated or it is growing too fast.

Rising inflation has an tenuous effect-input prices are higher, consumers can purchase fewer goods, revenues and profits decline, the entire economy slows for a time until monetary policies enter in the game.

There are monetary policies used by Central Banks to avoid changes of prices.

They raise the interest rates or reduce the supply of money in economy to reduce inflation, because it can lead to increased uncertainty and negative consequences of price changes for different levels in economy.

It impacts the corporate profits through higher input costs.

The company starts worrying about its future and stops hiring or starts firing employees from their jobs, making an impact in the standard of living of individuals, in their fixed income. Investors won't consider investing in a company which is not performing well in the period of inflation.

The falling in price of stocks indicates lower profitability for companies, the chance of unemployment and weaker economy.

When a person buys a share of stocks, she obtains a claim on current and future profits of a company. The price paid for that profit stream fastens the stock's rate of return to the owner per dollar invested. The more someone pays for a stream of real profits, the lower her or his real rate of return.

Several studies, during the past four decades have showed that there is a strong link between stock prices and business wealth. When the level of inflation was accelerating, the stock prices were falling and vice versa.

There is a tendency for stocks to decline when the inflation worsens because inflation affects the profitability of the company.

If the profitability of the company declines with higher inflation, investors will be less willing to supply companies with the funds needed to update their building and machines for production.

This will lead to slow growth in the economy's capacity to produce goods and provide services.

The government will respond with fiscal policies to in order to mitigate inflation's effects. This means to adjust parts of the tax code that allow inflation to harm equity values.

Expected inflation can either positively or negatively impact stocks, depending on the ability to hedge/confine and monetary policy.

Unexpected inflation studies have showed that there is a firm positive correlation between this type of inflation and the stock returns during economic decline. The timing of the economic cycle is very important for investors to foresee the impact on stock returns.

The unexpected inflation gives strong information about the future prices of the stocks.

It was discovered that the greater volatility (it indicates how quickly the value of an investment changes) of stock movements was linked to higher inflation rates.

All depends on the policies and decisions of the company.

Liquidity Risk

Investors are very concerned about the liquidity risk. The liquidity risk is the risk that a given security or asset cannot be traded quickly enough in the market to prevent a loss or make the required profit.

It harms their ability to trade the quantity of stocks they want to buy or sell in a short and desired period of time.

They fear that an event as a financial crisis will not be able exit the market fast enough to avoid losses.

The manifestation of liquidity risk is very different from a drop in price to zero. In case of a drop of an asset's price to zero, the market considers the asset worthless.

However, there are situations when one party can't find another party interested in trading the asset,

******

Unlike a bond, which promises a payout at the end of a specified period and an interest during the contract, the only assured return from a stock is if it appreciates on the open market.

Chapter 6

The Capital Asset Price Model

The Capital asset pricing model is an economic theory that promulgates the relationship between risk and expected return (a tool that determines whether an investment has a positive or negative average net outcome) and contributes as a model for the pricing of risky securities.

It assumes that the only risk that is priced by rational investors is the systematic risk because it can't be erased by the diversification of the investments portofolio.

The CAPM reason is to compensate investors' decision on investing their cash in two ways:

1. Time-value of money is represented by the risk-free rate and compensates investors by placing their money over a period of time.

2. Risk determines the amount of compensation the investor needs for taking an additional risk.

This is calculated by taking the risk measure-beta and the market premium-Rm-rf.

$Rc = Rf + \beta s (Rm-Rf)$

Rc=rate cost of equity

Rf= risk-free asset return rate

Bs (Rm-Rf)= risk premium

Bs= sensitivity coefficient

Rm-Rf=systematic risk prime

Rm= average profitability rate

The definition of Beta

Beta is a numeric value that measures the fluctuations of a stock to shifts in the overall stock market.

It evaluates the responsiveness of a stock's price to fluctuations in the overall stock market, helping the investor to decide whether he wants to invest in a riskier stock which is highly correlated with the market, having a beta above 1 or with a less volatile stock, with a beta below 1.

The market has a beta of 1. 0 and individual stocks are categorized according to how much they deviate from the market.

A beta above 1. 0 indicates that the stock is swinging more than the market over time.

If a stock oscillates less than the market, the beta's stock is less than 1. 0.

The theory is very simple: high-beta stocks are riskier but also provide potential for higher returns while low-beta stocks represent less risk but also lower returns.

It is a fundamental element of capital asset pricing model   (CAPM), which is used to calculate the cost of equity.

Fundamental Analysis Techniques

The fundamental analysis is the primary way and the most popular of studying the evolution of stocks.

Many investors use this approach. They look at the basic information about a company-growth of its sales and profits-trying to figure out what they consider the true or fair value of the company's stock.

Comparing the current stock price with the fair value, investors can determine if it might be a good time to buy that stock or if it's a stock to avoid.

Investors who use the fundamental analysis are focused on two distinct approaches to choosing stocks: growth or value or a combination of both.

Growth Stocks

Looking for the Sprinters

A growth stock is a stock of a company that generates considerable and sustainable positive cash flow and whose revenues and earnings are expected to rise at a faster rate than the average company within the same industry.

A growth company has some sort of competitive advantage. It outperforms its competitors through highly skilled personnel, new technologies, maybe low costs in that industry, a revolutionary product, a breakthrough patent, overseas expansion.

Investors who are focused on growth, try to discover or forecast which companies will grow faster in the future- faster than the rest of the stocks in the market or faster than other stocks in the same industry.

If an investor makes a good choice, buying stocks in a company that grows faster than other companies, then it's likely that the price of the company's stocks will rise as well and he can make profit.

A company that grows faster than the average usually pay few or no dividends, since they are more focused in reinvesting their profits in their business, in order to expand/grow it.

Individuals who decide to invest in growth stocks prefer them because their investment portofolio will be made up of established, well-managed companies that can be held onto for many years.

Examples of growing companies are IBM, Microsoft, Apple INC. , Coca-Cola. They have demonstrated great growth over the years and are the milestones of many investment portofolios.

Value Stocks

Chasing the Hidden Treasures

alue stocks are stocks that tend to trade at a lower price relative to its fundamental-dividends, earnings, sales and they are considered undervalued by a value investor.

These companies may have been beaten down in price because they have encountered bad events or may be in an industry that has been neglected by most investors.

However, even a company that has seen its stock price downturn still has assets to its name: buildings, subsidiaries, machines, real estate, inventories.

They may have a great value which may be not reflected in the stocks' price.

Value investors are looking for stocks that are undervalued.

Then they buy and keep them until the stock market realizes the real value of the company's assets.

One of the greatest investors of history, Warren Buffet is well known for his tendency in buying stocks, guided by the value approach.

Growth Vs. Value Stocks

Who's the winner?

Valuation starts and ends with profits. The faster a company's earnings grow and the more reliable they are, the more investors will pay for its stocks.

There is a set in stone rule in investing: everyone wants to buy low and sell high.

There are two approaches/strategies that determine the investors' choices: **growth** and **value**.

Growth investors are focused on investing in stocks with above-average earnings growth no matter what the price.

Value investors are hunting bargains or stocks that are trading at a discount to their usual valuation.

Value investors are concerned with here and now because they look for stocks that, at this moment, are trading for less than their real worth.

Growth investors are interested in the future potential of a company, with much less accent on its present price.

Which strategy is the most effective?

Most financial analysts and investors believe that value approach is highly effective, especially for long-term investors.

If an investor buys stocks at a relative low price to others, his returns benefit over time.

Let's suppose that an investor is looking to buy stocks that are typically traded in a P/E range between 20 and 30. If he buys them at 20 and let them move up to 19 before selling them, he will clearly see a bigger profit than if he buys them at 29 and let them move up to 30, then sells when they start to head back down.

Even if he ignores the short-time cycles and holds them for long-term, he is better off if he buys the stocks as cheaply as possible in the first place.

The ideal stock will have a low P/E and a fast rate of earnings growth, but these situations are rare because every time an opportunity like this appears, the price is boosted because of investors' high demand.

The success of an investments portofolio stands in the ability of investors to build a balanced portofolio of stocks.

They shouldn't miss the opportunity to own big, important companies like Microsoft, but they shouldn't pay too much for them either. The key is to find out when it's the perfect time to buy.

Technical Analysis

Technical analysis is the polar opposite of fundamental analysis, which is the foundation of the value and growth method.

Technical analysts or technicians select stocks by analyzing statistics generated by past market activity, prices and volume (the number of shares that trade hands during a single day) and other factors.

John Murphy explains in his book "Charting Made Easy" the basic premises and tools of the technical analysis called also chart analysis:

"Chart analysis is the study of market action, using price charts, to forecast future price direction. The cornerstone of the technical philosophy is the belief that all factors that influence market

price- fundamental information, political events, natural disaster, and psychological factors-are quickly discounted in the market activity.

In other words, the impact of these external factors will quickly show up in some form of price movement, either up or down".

By plotting and mathematical analysis, technical analysts want to predict future changes in the price of particular stocks.

They analyze the particular patterns on the price chart of stocks and try to discover the direction of the stock's price in the future.

These patterns have various names such as:" cup and handle", "head and shoulders" and "double top". If an analyst identifies different patterns on the analyzed stock, he will technically discover if the stock is about to "breakout" which means to rise in price or "retreat" which means to fall in price.

There are three assumptions technical analysts techniques are based upon:

1.   Prices reflect suggestive information. The stock market is very efficient.
2.   Prices move in trends.
3.   The history repeats itself.

The "cup and handle" pattern

This pattern marks the consolidation period followed by a breakout.

There are two parts: the cup and the handle.

The cup has the shape of "U" and it is formed after an advance. As the cup is completed, a trading scale develops on the right hand side and that is the handle.

A succeeding breakout from the handle's trading scale notifies the extension of the prior advance.

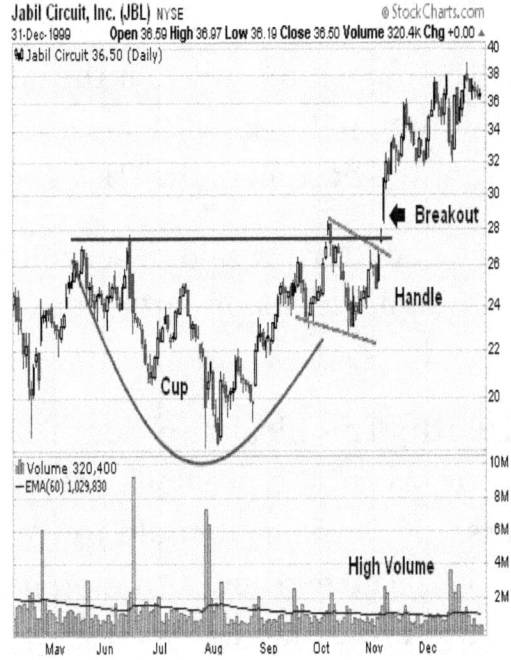

Trend: The continuation of a pattern can't be qualified without the existence of a prior trend. The trend should be only few months old or not too mature. The more mature the trend, the less evidence that the pattern indicated a continuation or the less upside potential.

Cup: The cup should have the "U" shape. The "V" shape bottom is too sharp. The softer "U" shape indicates that the cup is a consolidation pattern with a conclusive support at the bottom of the "U".

The perfect pattern would be a symmetric cup, with equal highs on both sides of the cup.

Cup Depth: The ideal cup depth should be 1/3 or less of the previous advance. In the versatile markets, it could range from 1/3 or 1/2. The extreme situation has the maximum retracement of 2/3.

Handle: It signifies the final consolidation before the big breakout and it can measure up 1/3 of the cup's advance, but no more than this.

The smaller the retracement, the more significant the breakout.

Duration: The cup duration is from 1 to 6 months. The handle varies from 1 week to many weeks.

Volume: There should be a considerable increase on the breakout above the handle's resistance.

Target: The designed advance after a breakout can be estimated by measuring the distance from the right peak of the cup to the bottom of the cup.

The "head and shoulders" pattern

The head and shoulders pattern is a reversal pattern. It points out that the security is likely to turn against the previous trend.

There are two versions of this pattern.

The head and shoulders top is a signal that a security's price is set to fall, once the pattern is completed. It is usually formed at the peak of an upward trend.

The other version is **the head and shoulders bottom** and it is the reverse of the first one. It signifies that a security's price is going to rise and it usually forms a downward trend.

Head and Shoulders Bottom

Neckline

Price

Left Shoulder

Right Shoulder

Head

Period & volume

The "double top" pattern

The double-top pattern can be found at the peaks of an upward trend. It highlights that the preceding upward trend is weakening and that buyers are losing interest.

A double top occurs when prices form two different peaks on the chart.

The first part of the pattern is the creation of a new high during the upward trend, which, after reaching the peak, confronts the resistance and sells off to a level of support (the price level which a stock has had difficulty falling below. It is the level at which a lot of buyers tend to buy that stock.)

The following stage of the pattern is formed when the price starts to move back towards the level of resistance found in the previous run-up, which again sells off back to the support level.

The pattern is completed when the security falls below the support level, marking the beginning of a downward trend.

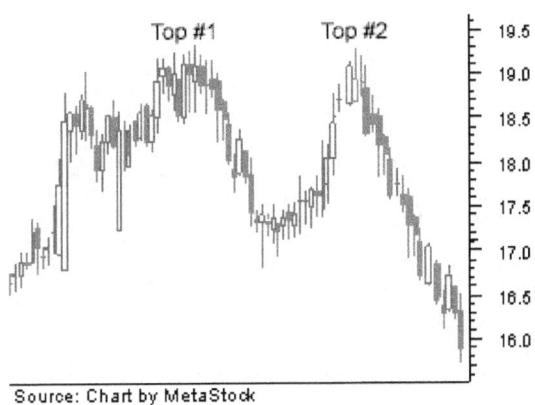

Source: Chart by MetaStock

This is the most common pattern used by analysts. Even if it is the most simple, it should be approached with caution by investors.

Many investors believe that the pattern is consistently reliable due to its double top. But it is not true. This pattern is believed to have a failure rate of 65%.

They should consider the volume during the formation of the pattern, the amount of decline between the two peaks and the time the pattern takes to grow on the chart.

This pattern forms usually in active market, facing heavy trading. The price of the stocks rises quickly in high volume.

The demand decreases and the price falls.

Another increase in price comes, taking the price back up to the level achieved by the first top.

In the second stage, the volume is heavy but not as in the first stage. Prices fall back again, unable to puncture the resistance level.

The last stage is meant to saturate the buying power of the stock. Left without power, the stock reverses its upward movement, falling into the downward trend.

Another way to analyze the evolution of stocks is the chart with the price history. The average price of the stock is calculated every day for the past 90 or 200 days. The moving average is plotted on the chart alongside the price and it will give you a clear perspective about the past trends of stocks' price.

Investing is not so hard if you master the technical analysis and you get access to charting software and price data.

The main tool in technical analysis is the stocks' price chart. So, once someone decides to invest, he has to vigilantly follow the performance of his investment in stocks.

Momentum Investing

The momentum investing is one of the techniques of picking stocks.

If you have been in the situation of parking your car on a hill and you forgot to set the brake, you will possibly know how quickly a moving automobile can pick up speed. That's the way some stocks moves.

Momentum investors dig for stocks that are moving at high speeds. They buy them when they continually rise in price and sell them before they crash or burn.

Investors appreciate momentum in one of two basic ways, by considering the performance of the earnings of the company or the company's price.

Momentum investors predict that companies with the major prices changes over the most recent few months are poised to continue making high gains.

Momentum investing is based on companies with fast growing earnings, more than 30% a year or more.

There is a huge risk in investing in these stocks because they are already known on the stock market, the have a high price and P/E ratio and their price can drop very quickly when the earnings are disappointing and they are punished.

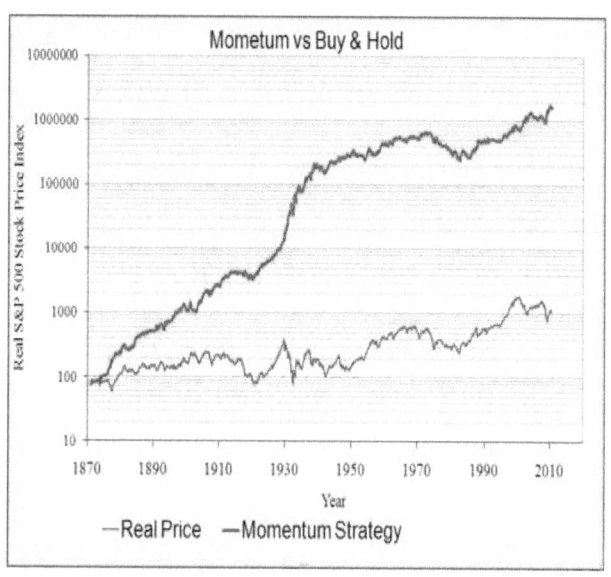

Online Investing

The greatest word that describes the stock market is the word "fast".

The price of stocks, especially high tech stocks can soar and drop suddenly. That fast market is full of investors who want to trade at the same time because prices change faster.

There will be always delays in the process of investing, because changes of price happen too fast and the report lag behind actual prices.

Due to these delays, investors can suffer unexpected losses too quickly.

Online investors have to be well prepared for dealing with fast growing markets and also understand their mechanism.

There are two ways of avoiding or limiting their losses in fast moving markets:

1.   Knowing what they are buying and the risk of their investment
2.   Knowing the mechanism of fast markets and how trading changes in these markets. Protecting their investment from typical problems that can occur in these markets.

Online investing is easy and fast.

There is one click that separates you from buying stocks at a low prices and selling them at the highest price on the market.

Even if online trading saves investors time and money, there is something that requires time –making a wise investment decision.

Before trading, every investor should know the potential and the risk of his investment.

They need to set the price limits on fast moving stocks.

In order to avoid buying a stock at a higher price or selling one at a lower price than the market price, investors should **set a limit order** rather than a market order.

What does it mean?

A limit order is an order to buy or sell a security at a specific price.

A buy limit order can be executed only at a limit or lower. A limit sell order can be executed only at a limit price or higher.

If the investor sets a market order, he won't be able to control the price at which his order will be executed.

Another mistake of the online investors is that they place an order and they assume it didn't go through, so they end up owning twice as much stock they should afford or wanted or selling more than they have had.

If an investor decides to cancel an order, he should check if the order was cancelled before placing another trade.

In conclusion, the stock is the equity stake of its owner. For a company, it represents the residual asset that would be due to stockholders after discharge of all senior claims (secured and unsecured debt).

The share is the portion of a corporation stock, the total of which is stated at the business formation.

They represent a fraction of ownership in a business. The ownership rules, privileges and share values depend on the business. The ownership of shares is certified by the issuance of a stock certificate (a legal document that certifies the ownership of a specific number of stocks in a company).

The enormous factory called stock market lets investors participate in the financial accomplishments of the companies whose shares they hold.

When companies enjoy the success, stock market investors make money through the dividends the companies pay out and by selling appreciated stocks at a profit called a capital gain.

The hindrance is that investors can lose money of the companies whose stocks they hold lose money, the stocks' price falls and the investor sells the stock at a loss.

The success of an investment depends on the ability of the investor to predict changes in the stock market, analyzing different ratios and making decisions based on real information.

Breaking the rules without any risk

The majority of professional long term investors have adjusted a shorter term view when seeking for earning opportunities in an inefficient market.

They assume that the market is not always able to immediately assimilate into the price all substantial information and they search for undervalued securities to purchase.

They hope to make profit when the undervalued securities' prices settle down to the real fair market values. But it may or may not happen during the process.

They goal is to capitalize on short-term price movements extruding in and out the volatile market, buying and selling what they consider as undervalued securities with noteworthy frequency.

In short, the amazing majority of professional investors focus on short-term investments, having a short-sighted view of the market actively pursuing investing opportunities and timing their trades with the use of self-serving technical analysis tools with the purpose of outperforming the market.

Their perspective about the market is inefficient compared to the theory of the efficient market which states that the market always factors into the price all relevant information about the security, as they occur and when they occur, without any delay.

The securities are always valued correctly and they will never be undervalued or overvalued based on fundamental information underlying the particular securities.

To consider a security as undervalued or overvalued in relation to a conceived future fair value is therefore downright abstract, speculative and unfounded.

This is the reason why the performance of most of these professional investors who actively handle their investments always collapses way below actual market returns.

Only 20% of these investors manage to outperform the corresponding market indexes while the rest pathetically lag the market.

But they still continue to actively follow their investing strategy and they trade their accounts, time the market and search for undervalued assets.

The most appropriate way to outperform them is to do the opposite of what they are doing: creating a good, long-term strategy, one that will continue to be resilient during bad times and at the same time able to monetize during thriving times.

Think about the performance of company. A successful company is the result of long-term directions and decisions implemented by a strategic leader or manager, whose aim is to create, fortify and develop the objectives and mechanisms of the company, that lead to high achievements, based on a long-term strategy.

Now think about your strategy.

In order to achieve success, you need to build a long-term strategy. You will probably divide it in short-term goals, only to make it more achievable, but you need to imagine the entire process, the big picture of your investing decision, then to think about your small steps that lead to the achievement of the big goal.

Building Long-Term Strategies

Long-term investing strategies involves blending a mix of a less risky and less volatile securities which most investors normally hesitate because of what they consider as their laggard performance.

Long-term strategies require investing time and patience before they start to deliver the desired results.

However, over time, they will bring you more returns than the more volatile securities which active traders are fond of.

Studies made by Russell Investments showed that the more volatile securities, with a higher Beta, generated lower returns than the less risky, less volatile securities over time.

There are some fundamental concepts you should know as an investor.

First one, you should definitely sell the losers from your portofolio and let the winners ride.

What does it mean? Investors were used to take profits from selling their appreciated investments and hold the stocks that have declined in the hope of a rebound.

If an investor doesn't know when it's the time to sell those hopeless stocks, he can reach that level where the stock is almost worthless.

Maybe this theory sounds great, but it's hard to put into practice.

Riding a winner might be a great strategy, but you need to have a good understanding of the potential of your investments.

Peter Lynch is famous for his investment that increases tenfold in value.

His overall success is based on a small number of stocks in his portofolio that returned big.

His core thesis highlights three fundamental tenets:

1. Only buy what you understand

He always believed that the greatest stock research tools are his eyes, ears and the common sense.

He discovered most of his stock ideas while through the grocery store or chatting with his family or friends.

We are all able to analyze these things at the first glance. We are all consumers of goods and services.

The idea is that most of the stock market is in the business of serving you as a consumer. If that good or service attracts you as a consumer, then it should also attract your interest as an investment.

2. Always do your homework

Every first-hand observation is a great start, but the amazing ideas need to be followed by a smart and detailed research.

The rigorous research was the cornerstone of Peter Lynch's success.

He had found the following values as fundamental for a stock worth buying:

I. Percentage of sales

If there is a product or service that attracts you to the company, make sure that it brings a high percentage of sales to that company. If it brings only 10% of sales, it won't have more than a marginal impact on a company's bottom line (a company's net earnings/net income or earnings per share-EPS but it also refers to the actions that increase or decrease the net earnings of the overall profit of the company).

II. EG Ratio (Price/Earnings to Growth Ratio)

Analyzing this indicator, the investor will see how much expectation is built into the stock. The companies with strong earnings growth and considerable valuations are those with a high PEG ratio. It provides a powerful analysis about the valuation of those stocks, a more complete picture than simply analyzing the price-earnings ratio-P/E.

III.   Prefer always companies with a powerful cash position and below-average debt-to- equity ratios because those companies have an outstanding potential and they make investments with prudency.

3.   Invest for a long-run.

Lynch considered the short –term investing as a loss of time. He didn't try to predict short-run fluctuations of the market because he believed that if the company is strong, he will earn more and the stock will appreciate in value over time. He had spent his time chasing great companies, with huge potential and credibility.

The second concept is to sell the losers from your portofolio, because there is no guarantee that a stock will bounce back after a long-winded decline.

It is important not to undervalue good stocks, but also it is important to be realistic about investments that are not performing very well.

A market research is necessary when establishing the real potential of a stock.

Thirdly, as a long-term investor, you should not panic when your investment experience short-term movements.

In a long-run investment, the big picture is the most suggestive one. The short-term volatility doesn't reflect the quality of your investment.

Another aspect, never overestimate the few cents difference you have saved from using a limit versus market order.

Active traders use these day-to-day or minute-to-minute fluctuations as a manner of making profit. But they won't make too much profit from short-run investments. But the gains of a long-term investor come from a completely different perspective and market movement. These gains come from years of focus on your investment and development of a strong investing philosophy, they come from educating yourself.

The forth concept is based on picking a strategy and sticking with it.

There are different investors that use different methods of choosing stocks and fulfill their investing aims.

There are many ways to be successful and no one strategy is better than any other.

But, once you have found your strategy, stick with it. If an investor oscillates between different stock-picking strategies, he will probably get the worst, rather than the best achievements, for each strategy.

The fifth concept is about focusing on the future.

The resilient part about investing is that we are trying to take informed decisions based on facts that have yet to happen.

Even if we use past data as an indicator for feasible future performance, it is what happens in the future that matters most.

The secret of a successful investment is to base the investing decision on the future potential than on what has already happened in the past.

The point is to check the fundamentals of a company before taking the risk of investing in its stocks.

The sixth concept is about adopting a long-term perspective.

Large short-term profits can be achieved buy new investors on the stock market. But adopting a long-term outlook is a must for any investor. As an investor, you need to avoid the antique mentality of "getting in, getting out and making a killing". It doesn't work too long.

It doesn't mean that you can't make a huge amount of money by actively trading, but trading and investing are very different in principles and perspectives. They are different ways of achieving gains from the market.

For those with high experience, knowledge and desire to create wealth, investing is the right choice.

Part III

Bond Investing

A small overview of bonds

A bond is an interest-bearing certificate, issued by government agencies (treasury bonds, agency bonds or municipal bonds) or private corporations (corporate bonds).

The bond market, named also debt or credit market, is a financial environment where the issuance and trading of debt securities occurs.

The bond market primarily comprises government-issued securities and corporate debt securities.

This market makes possible the transfer of capital from savers to the issuers or organizations that requires capital for starting government projects, expanding their business or ongoing operations.

The government bond market is the largest part of the bond market, due to its size and liquidity.

The bond market in her complexity is driven by the same risk and return tradeoffs as the stock market.

The broader bond market is divided in five specific bond markets.

1.   Corporate

It is a bond issued by a corporation with the aim of financial raise for a diversity of reasons such as ongoing operations or the expansion the business.
They are usually applied to longer-term debt instruments, with a maturity-final payment date of at least one year.

Corporate debt instruments with the maturity shorter than a year are mentioned as commercial papers.

The corporate bonds are traded in decentralized, dealer-based, over-the-counter markets.

In this type of market- over-the counter, the trading dealers play a intermediary role between buyers and sellers.

If you didn't know it, the largest, the oldest, most developed market for corporate bonds is the US Dollar corporate bond market.

The size of the market fluctuates according to who is doing the counting, from $5 to $6 trillion range.

The second largest corporate bond market from the world is the Euro denominated corporate market.

Other markets are not so well-developed and they have small trading volumes.

The main categories of corporate bonds:

The corporate bonds are divided into two main categories according to their credit rating (the bond credit rating is the credit worthiness of the corporate or government bonds. It is published by the Credit rating agencies and they are used by professional investors to figure out the probability for the debt to be repaid.)

I.   **High Grade** (Investment Grade) - are issued by large and very creditworthy corporations with high credit ratings.

The Standard& Poor's credit rating agencies assigns bond credit ratings of AAA, AA, A, BBB and they represent the quality of the bond.

Moody's credit rating agency assigns bond credit ratings of Aaa, Aa, A, Baa.

High Grade corporate bonds assure a slightly higher stream of income than government bonds because they are not guaranteed by the government.

The difference in rate between corporate and government bonds increases and falls as an outcome of investor confidence, investors' willingness to assume a risk, the expectation for the economy and growth in corporate profits.

These rates or interest-rate spreads are indicators of the rates between distinct types of bonds.

The risk for the investment grade corporate bonds is very low. The only risk investors assume is that the issuing company might not be able to make its interest and principal payments.

II.   **High-Yield** (Non-Investment Grade Speculative Grade, Junk Bonds) - are issued by corporations that don't have the same high credit ratings as high grade issuers.

The Standard& Poor's credit rating agencies assigns bond credit ratings of BB, B, CCC, CC, C, D for high yield corporate bonds.

Moody's credit rating agency assigns high-yields corporate bonds credit ratings of Ba, B, Caa, Ca, C.

During the history, they have provided a higher yield for investors than investment-grade corporate or government bonds, because the higher yield compensates the risk of the issuing company not making its interest and principal payments.

The high risk is the fundamental aspect you should know about the high-yield corporate bonds. Investing in this type of corporate bonds, you take the risk of not getting your money back.

The risk valuation of corporate bonds

Compared to government bonds, corporate bonds have a higher risk of default (the risk of default is the failure of meeting the legal obligations of a loan).

There are many factors that influence the risk of default: the particular corporation issuing the bond, the current market conditions and governments to which the bond issuer is being compared and also the rating of the company.

The higher yield than government bonds is the compensation for the risk assumed by corporate bond holders.

The interest rate risk:

Like all bonds, the corporate bonds tend to increase their value when the interest rates fall and they fall in value when interest rates rise.

The longer the maturity of a corporate bond, the greater the degree of price volatility.

This means that if you hold a bond until maturity, you will be less concerned about the price fluctuations, known as interest rate risk or market risk, because you will get the par value of the bond at maturity.

Many investors get confused because of the inverse relationship between bonds and interest rates. The idea is that a bond becomes worthless when the interest rates rise.

When the interest rates rise, new issues appear on the market with higher yields than the older securities and this determine the decrease in price of the old ones, so they become worthless.

When the interest rates decline, new bonds are issued with lower yields than older securities, determining the older, higher yielding one worth. Their price will go up.

There are various economic powers that affect the level and the direction of the interest rate in the entire economy.

The interest rate rises when the economy is growing and falls during the economic recessions.

Inflation is one of the most influential elements on interest rates.

When the inflation is rising, interest rates rise too. When the inflation is moderated, interest rates are lower.

Liquidity risk:

The liquidity risk represents the risk of having insufficient buyers or seller to promote or encourage trade in the open market.

Bonds are sold in the primary market, directly from issuers when they are first issued.

They can be traded in the secondary market only before their maturity date.

Liquidity of a bond means the effortlessness with which a bond can be bought or sold in the secondary market.

The size and the turnover volume of the secondary market influence and affect the liquidity of the bonds.

If there are enough buyers and sellers in the market to stimulate trading of a bond, it will be considered more liquid.

There is a general rule for bond liquidity which states that bonds with higher credit rating are usually more liquid.

A bond with a higher credit rating is more attractive and has a more substantial trading volume, even in times of market constraint when investors are more risk hostile.

The investment grade bonds are more resilient to liquidity risk than non-investment grade bonds.

How currencies affect the liquidity of a bond:

Currencies play a fundamental role in determining the liquidity of a bond.

Bonds which are denominated in major currencies, such as the USD and JPY tend to magnetize more foreign investments.

The reason why currencies influence the liquidity of the bonds is because the major currencies are more commonly traded internationally and the bonds denominated in these currencies usually have more active secondary markets.

The bonds denominated in the emerging-market currencies experience higher liquidity risk.

How liquidity can influence the price of bonds:

Liquidity can influence and affect the price of trading of bonds.

The more liquid a bond it, the greater the ability to respond to the market shifts.

With enough participant and settled trading volume in the marker, bonds can be traded without bringing major ruptures to the market price.

The illiquid bonds have an insufficient market participants and demand, so they respond less quickly to market events.

How investors can manage the liquidity risk:

In order to administrate the liquidity risk, investors should consider investing in the more liquid assets, such as investment grade bonds.

Another escape is to invest in a diversified portofolio which is made up of single bonds issued by distinct issuers.

It might require a notable investment amount to reach such level of diversification given the high minimum investment threshold in single bond investments.

Another way of managing the liquidity risk is to invest in a single bond investments or a bond fund.

Bond funds may increase with 40-plus underlying assets issued by distinct entities globally or regionally to achieve diversification.

2.   Government and Agency Bonds

A government bond is a debt security issued by a government to stimulate and support the government spending, most often issued in the country's domestic currency.

Government debt is money owed by any level of government and Is backed by the full trust of the government.

They are made with the promise of paying periodic interest payments and repay the face value on the maturity date.

Government bonds are free of credit risk because the government can raise taxes or simply print more money to ransom the bond at maturity. But they are not risk-free! But investing in this type of bonds requires the knowledge of country risk, political risk, inflation risk and interest rate risk.

The federal government bonds in United States of America include:

- **Saving bonds** are debt securities issued by the U. S. Department of Treasury to support pay for the U. S. government borrowing needs.

They are considered one of the safest investments because they are backed by the full faith and credit of the U. S. government.

They are issued in eight values: $50, $75, $100, $200, $500, $1000, $5000, $10000.

If an investor decides to buy this type of bonds, he must wait at least six month before chasing it in, when they will receive the capital plus interests.

The maturity date for saving bonds varies, but the longer you wait, the greater interest you earn.

If you want to purchase these bonds, you need to register Treasury Direct account. It requires a social security number, a driver's license, a checking or savings account and an email address.

Many investors find this type of investment very attractive because they are not the subject to state or local income taxes.

- **Treasury bonds** are marketable, fixed-interest U. S. government debt securities with a maturity range of 10 to 30 years and they are available in increments of $100.

The interest payments are made semi-annually and the income that holders receive is only taxed at the federal level.

Treasury bonds can be purchased directly from the U. S. Treasury or through participating banks or brokers.

The bonds are sold in an auction that sets the price and the yield of the bond.

There are two types of bids for purchasing a treasury bond:

1.   Non-competitive bid, where the bidder agrees to accept the rate decided in the auction. This guarantees that the bidder can buy the bond, but he must pay the full amount.

2.   Competitive bid, where the bidder decides an acceptable yield.

There are three options.

If the bid is equal to or less than the yield, the bid is accepted at its full price.

If the bid is equal to the high bid of the auction, the bid is accepted at less than the full amount bid.

If the yield requested is higher than the yield set at the auction, the bid is rejected. The maximum a bidder can purchase depends on the type of bid from the auction.

For a non-competitive bid, the maximum is $5000000 per security type, term and auction.

For competitive bids, the maximum is 30% of the offering amount.

- **Treasury inflation-protected security** is a treasury security indexed to inflation in order to protect investors from the negative effects of inflation.

The inflation adjustment is made on the semi-annual basis. The adjustment is made to the bond's par value rather than the interest rate. Adjusting the bond this way, not only protects the bond's interest payment from inflation, but also protects the bond's face value.

In order to understand the process, let's suppose than an investor purchases a $1000 TIPS from the U. S. Treasury with a 4% fixed interest rate. Assumed that the inflation, which is measured by the Consumer Price Index, is 12% for the first year of this bond, at the beginning of the second year, the bond's face value will be adjusted by 12%, $1120.

The 4% interest will then be paid on this new face value amount.

The internal revenue service considers an adjustment to a security's face value as taxable income, even though investors don't see the money until they sell the bond or it reaches maturity.

This is why many investors prefer to invest in TIPS mutual funds or hold the TIPS in tax-deferred retirement accounts, in order to avoid tax complications.

They are an extremely low-risk investment because they are sustained by the U. S. government and also their par value rises with the inflation, while their interest rate stands fixed. They are also free from state and local income taxes.

The fixed interest rate for the treasury inflation-protected bonds is paid semiannually.

They can be purchased directly from the government, through the Treasury Direct system. The minimum investment is $1000 and it comes in $100 increments. The maturity range is from 5 to 30 years.

3.   **Municipal bond** is a debt security issued by a state, municipality or county to subsidize its capital expenditures (the construction of highways, bridges, schools, public housing, sewer, power utilities, hospitals, water systems).

They provide tax relief from federal taxes and local taxes. They consist in short-term issues named called notes, which have their maturity in one year or less, and long-term issues named bonds, which mature in more than one year.

The called notes are used by the issuer to increase money for a variety of reasons, in anticipation of future revenues such as taxes, state or federal aid payments and future bond issuances.

They also can cover some irregular cash-flows, meet unanticipated deficits or raise immediate capital for projects until the long-term financing can be ordered.

Bonds are used to finance capital projects over the longer term.

The municipal bonds are divided into two main categories:

• General obligation bond or full-faith-and-credit bond is a municipal debt obligation on which the interest and the principal are guaranteed by the full financial resources and taxing power of the issuer.

• Revenue bond is a bond issued by the municipality to finance a project or an enterprise in which the issuer pledges to the bondholders the revenues warranted by the operation of the projects financed. Conclusive examples are the hospital revenue bonds or the sewer revenue bonds.

The municipal bonds bear interest at a variable or fixed rate of interest.

The process of issuing bonds is governed by an extensive system of regulations and laws, which are chosen by each state.

The issuer of the municipal bonds gets cash payment in the moment of issuance in exchange for the promise to repay the investors who provide money (bond holder) over time.

The repayments periods varies from few months to 20, 30, 40 years or longer.

The issuer uses revenues/proceeds from the bond sale to pay for the capital projects or for other purposes it cannot pay immediately with funds on hand.

The tax regulations for the municipal bonds claim that all money earned from a bond sale to be spent on one-time capital projects within three to five years or issuance.

The municipal bonds can be purchased directly from the issuer (primary market) or from other bond holder at some time after issuance (secondary market).

In exchange for the capital investment, the bond holder will receive payments over time, comprising the interest on the invested principal and a return of the invested principal itself.

The interest (coupon) for municipal bonds is paid semi-annually.

The main reason municipal bonds are considered separately from other types of bonds is their ability to bring tax-relief income.

The interest paid by the issuer to bond holder is relieved from federal, local or state taxes. But there are some restrictions and they depend on the state in which the issuer is located. Some bonds have a minimum tax for their interest.

For example, the interest earning on bonds that fund projects that are created for the public good are free from federal income tax, while those issued with the purpose of funding projects partly of wholly benefiting only private parties, named also private activity bonds, are the subject of federal income tax.

However, qualified private activity bonds, which are issued by the governmental units or private entities, are free from federal taxes because they finance service or facilitate them and, while meeting the private activity tests are needed by the government.

Risk of municipal bonds:

The type of risk depends on the type of bond, because every type is secured by another repayment source, based on the promise made in the bond documents. Based on the source of their interest payments and principal payments, municipal bonds are divided into:

- **General obligation bonds** are engaged to repay based on the full faith and credit of the issuer. They are the most secure type of municipal bond but they carry the lowest interest rate.

General obligation also means that the issuer has unlimited authority to tax residents to pay bondholders, but there are cases in which the issuer or the governmental entity may have limited or no taxing authority.

- **Revenue bonds** promise to repay from a specified stream of future income, such as the income generated by a water utility from payments by customers. The issuers of the revenue bonds are generally non-profit organizations, private-sector corporations and companies that provide a public service such as utilities or public transportation authorities.

The probability of repayment is determined by a rating agency for municipal bonds such as Standard & Poor's, Moody's and Fitch or by an independent reviewer.

They have a low rate of default because they are gauged by the revenue (revenue bonds) from public utilities, state and government power to tax (general obligation bonds).

4. Mortgage-backed, asset-backed, collateralized debt obligations

It is an asset-backed security that is secured by a mortgage or a manifold of mortgages.

The mortgages are sold to a government agency or an investment bank that packages the loans together into a security that is ready to be sold to an investor.

The most basic meaning of mortgage-backed securities –MBS is that homeowners' mortgage payments are passed through to the bondholder, in this way the bondholder receives monthly payments including the principal and the interest.

This is the main and key difference between MBS and other bonds such as Treasuries, where the interest is paid every six months and the whole principal at maturity.

There are several steps in creating a mortgage-backed security:

- A mortgage lender, such as a bank, spreads a loan to a homeowner.
- The mortgage lender sells the loan to a government-sponsored enterprise such as Fannie Mae or Freddie Mac, called Agencies or to a private entity, as a bank or finance company. In that moment, the lender still service the mortgage, making the process invisible to the homeowner.

- The Agency or the private entity takes a number of mortgage loans it has purchased and gathers them into a "pool". The number of mortgages from the pool can vary from few loans to thousands of loans. When homeowners pay their monthly payments, the pool of mortgages generates cash-flows regularly.

- The Agency or the private entity sells claims on that cash flow, in the form of securities-bonds for investors. After the primary sale, MBS trade on the open market.

- Then the mortgage payments, including the interest and the principal, are passed through the chain, from the entity to the bondholder.

Types of Mortgage-Backed Securities:

- **Pass-throughs** securities are also known as participation certificates and they are the most basic mortgage-backed bonds. They are collateralized by pools of similar mortgage loans. Most of them have the following issuers: Ginnie Mae, Fannie Mae or Freddie Mac and their cash flow is passed through to the MBS investor.

• **Collateralized Mortgage Obligations** are very different from pass-throughs, when talking about payments of principal and interest. Not all investors want to receive monthly payments of principal and interest that MBS pass-throughs offer. For this type of MBS, the cash flow are pooled and structured into many classes of securities with distinct maturities and payment schedules. The CMOs use pools of pass-throughs and or mortgage loans as collateral. There are three or more bond classes named tranches. Each tranche has its own expected maturity and cash flow pattern. The unique pattern for each type of CMOs tranche offers to investors the opportunity to tailor their mortgage exposure to meet a range of investment objectives, considering the distinct risk/return characteristic of the different classes. Some CMOs are very stable, with low-risk at investment while others are more volatile and risk laden.

- **Residential mortgage-backed security** is a pass-through MBS backed by mortgages on residential properties.

- **Commercial mortgage-backed security** is a pass-through MBS backed by mortgages on commercial properties.

- **Stripped mortgage-backed security** is quite different because each mortgage payment is partly used to pay the loans' principal and partly used to pay the interest on it. There are two types of stripped mortgage-backed securities: **interest-only stripped mortgage-backed securities**, a bond with cash flows backed by the interest component of the property owner's mortgage investment and the **principal-only stripped mortgage-backed security**, which is a bond with cash-flows backed by the principal repayment component of property owner's mortgage payments.

Mortgages backed securities are the largest segment of the U. S. Bond Market.

Mortgages are also among the most actively traded in the U. S. bond market.

The Ginnie Mae, Fannie Mae and Freddie Mac Agencies participate in the primary MBS market, which includes mortgages made to borrowers with strong credit histories.

The secondary mortgage market

The secondary market is the key element for maintaining the lender liquidity and also the efficiency of the loans.

This is the market where lenders sell and investors buy existing mortgages or MBS.

A wide percentage of the newly mortgages are sold by their originators into this large and liquid market, where they are securitized into MBS and sold to public and private investors, such as Fannie Mae, Freddie Mac, pension funds, insurance companies and mutual funds.

The main reason for retaining the lender liquidity is the long-term nature of mortgages.

The capital's infusion from investors purvey mortgage lenders such as banks, thrifts, mortgage bankers and other loan originators with a market for their loans.

The Covered Bonds Market

The covered bond market grants investors an alternative to advanced country government securities for bond investors, partisans of the most highly rated securities.

Covered bonds are renowned for the dual nature of protection offered to investors.

The covered bonds are securities created from public sector loans or mortgage loans where the security is backed by a separate group of loans.

They are backed by cash flows from mortgages or public sector loans.

Covered bonds are similar to asset-backed securities created in securitization, but they stay on the issuer's consolidated balance sheet (named also statement of financial position is a summary of the financial balances of s business partnership, corporation or other business organization. It contains the assets, liabilities and the ownership equity of a specific date, usually made at the end of the financial year).

Covered bonds are issued by financial institutions, mostly banks, which are responsible for their repayment.

They are also backed by a special pool of collateral, high-grades mortgages or loans to the public sector, on which the investors have a priority claim.

5. Bond fund

A bond fund includes mutual funds (open-end and closed end, actively managed and indexed), exchange traded fund (EFT) or unit investment trusts.

The come in many shapes and sizes and they are divided in some major categories, by their primary underlying assets:

- U. S. Treasury bond funds
- Municipal bond funds
- Corporate bond funds
- International bond funds
- Mixed

When an investor buys a bond fund, he actually buys shared in a portofolio of bonds that is designed or managed to pursue a specific investment objective such as current income, current tax-relief income, total return.

In the investment portofolio should be a particular type of bond- government, mortgage, municipal, high-yield or a particular maturity range (short-term- three years or less; intermediate term- three to 10 years; long-term- 10 years or longer).

The most important thing to know about bond funds is that they are composed of bonds, but they don't always act like bonds. Their payments are made quarterly or monthly, as apposed to the semunannual payments of bonds. The price is established using the Net Asset Value or the total market value of the portofolio divided by the total number of fund shares outstanding. Their price changes daily because of market factors.

This is because bond funds don't mature like individual bonds. Fund investors buy and sell bonds of differing maturities. This produces permanent shifts in their trading profits, losses and yields.

In spite of the fact that bond fund's investments mature, the fund's investors don't receive their original investments back until they sell their shares.

The advantages of investing in a bond fund are the low risk of the investment and the convenience of monthly payments. Diversification is a manner to avoid the often higher transaction costs and lower liquidity related to trading individual bonds.

The big disadvantage of mutual funds is that they have fluctuating share prices.

If an investor holds shares in a bond fund, he won't have the possibility to hold his investment until maturity, because he will try to avoid market-value loss. This is the opposite situation of individual bonds.

Types of Bond Funds

There are six types of bond funds and you are going to discover the characteristics of each type:

1.   Actively managed bond funds

Managers buy and sell bonds in pursuit of their investment objectives. They sell bonds at a profit, making a capital increase, or at a loss if they need money to pay their shareholders who want to sell their shares.

2.   Index bond funds

They are not actively managed by managers but there are created to fit the composition of a given bond index and when that index changes, the portofolio of investments changes automatically.

3.   Sponsors of open-end bond funds

They grant new shares and redeem existing shares constantly. They require their managers to invest cash coming into the fund and dissolve positions when they need cash to meet redemptions. Investors of open-end bond funds has to choose between collecting their interest income and capital gains or reinvest them automatically in new funds shares.

4. Closed-end bond funds

They have a fixed number of shares that trade on exchanges in the same way as stocks, at a price below or above net asset value, as a result of the demand and supply. They can be managed actively or indexed. In order to buy shares in a closed end fund, you have to consult a broker and pay a commission.

5. Exchanged Traded Funds (EFT)

They are marketable securities that track an index, a commodity, bonds or a basket of asset like an index fund. They are traded on an exchange, with shares bought or sold through a broker, where investors need to pay a commission.

6. Unit investment trusts

They are distinct portofolio of bonds held in a trust that sells a fixed number of shares. At the maturity date, the portofolio is liquidated and the proceeds are returned to unit holders on a pro rata basis.

Risks of bond funds

Interest rate risk

Bond funds returns are highly dependent on the changes in general interest rates.

So, when the interest rates increase, the value of bonds decrease, which affects the bond funds returns.

Credit Risk

The bond funds have the highest credit rating-"AAA".

Although most bond funds spread credit risk well enough, you should still understand that the weighted average credit rating of a bond fund will increase the volatility of it.

The weighted average credit rating is the weighted average of all the bond credit ratings in a bond fund. The measure provides for investors an idea of how risky a fund's bonds are overall. It is obtained by dividing the value of each bond in the fund by the total value of the fund.

This weight decides how much that bond affects the weighted average credit rating.

If a bond fund has 95% AAA government bonds and 5% junk bonds (non-investment bonds), the bond fund still have a weighted average credit rating of AAA.

The lower the weighted average credit rating, the riskier the bond funds. The weighted average credit rating is expressed as a letter rating AAA-the highest, BBB, CCC-the lowest.

Foreign Exchange Risk

The foreign currency exposure is another factor that determines the volatility in bonds.

It is a risk of an investment's value which fluctuates due to changes in currency exchange rates.

This affects the export or import, but also the investors who make international investments. This is because money have to be transformed to another currency in order to make an investment and any changes in the currency exchange rate causes the investment's value to decrease or increase when the investment is sold or converted back into the original currency.

This happens when a fund invests in bonds that are denominated in its domestic currency. This is because currencies are more volatile than bonds and the currency for a foreign currency bon can end up reducing the fixed-income return of the bond.

Strategies for Investing in Bonds

Have ever wondered how bond can work in order to fulfill you investment goals? Well, they have a range of investing strategies, from a buy-and-hold approach to more complex tactical trades that involve factors as inflation or interest rate.

Any investment goal is based on choosing the right strategy. The right strategy depends on your objectives, your time frame and your resistance and appetite to risk.

Investing in bonds can help you meet your financial goals: preserving principal, earning income, managing tax liabilities, balancing the risk of stock investments and growing your assets.

The most important aspect of a bond investment strategy is diversification.

There is a general rule which states that you should never put all your assets and all your risk in a single asset class or investment.

Diversification is defined through spreading the risk of your bond investments by creating a portofolio of several bonds, each with specific features.

Choosing bonds from distinct issuers protects you from the risk that any one issuer will be unable to respect its obligations to pay interest and principal.

Choosing bonds from different types-government, corporate, municipal, agency, mortgage-backed securities will protect yourself from losing in any particular market sector.

Including in your portofolio bonds with different maturity dates will help you manage the interest rate risk.

There is a wide range of strategies to follow to achieve your investment objectives:

Preserving Principal and Earning Interest

The buy and hold strategy is the most efficient strategy for those interested in keeping their money and earning interest.

When you invest in a bond and keep it until maturity, you get the interest payments, usually twice a year, and receive the face value of the bond at maturity.

One thing you should know: if you invest in a bond which is selling at a premium because its interest is higher than the prevailing interest rates, the amount you receive at maturity will be less than the amount you pay for the bond.

When you decide to follow this strategy, you should consider the impact of the interest rates on the bond's price or market value.

If the interest rate rises and the market value of the bond fall, you will not feel the effect of it unless you decide to change the strategy and sell the bond. Holding on to the bond means that you will not be able to reinvest the principal at the higher market rates.

If the bond you choose is callable, you should embrace the risk of having your principal returned before maturity. Bonds are called or redeemed by the issuers before maturity, when the interest rates are failing, so you will be forced to reinvest the returned principal at lower prevailing rates.

When choosing this strategy, you should consider many factors:

1.   **Coupon interest rate of the bond** (the yield paid by a fixed income security; it is calculated by dividing the sum of the security's annual coupon payments and dividing them by the bond's par value)

2.   **The yield to maturity or yield to call** because higher yields mean higher risks

3.   **The credit quality of the issuer**. A lower credit rating offers a higher yields but also a greater risk that the issuer will

not be able to pay the interest and the principal.

Maximizing Income

If the main objective of your investment in bonds is to maximize your income, then you will be more interested in getting higher coupons on longer-term bonds. Longer-term bonds have more time to maturity and they are more likely to change the interest rates.

The corporate bonds have higher coupon rates than U. S. treasury bonds with comparable maturities. In the bond market, corporate bonds with lower credit ratings pay higher income than higher-credits with comparable maturities.

High-yield bond, named also junk bonds, offer above-market coupon rates and yields because their issuers have credit rating below the investment grade-BB or lower. A low credit rating is linked to a greater risk because the issuer can default his obligations, being unable to pay the interest and the principal.

If an investor considers high-yield bonds as the primary element of his portofolio, he will also want to diversify the bond investment among several different issuers. This will help him minimize the effect of a single issuer's default. He should also consider that high-yield bonds' prices are more vulnerable at economic recessions or changes, when the risk of default is higher.

Managing Interest Rate Risk

Buy-and-hold investors discovered that they can manage the interest rate risk by creating an investment laddered (a portofolio with fixed-income securities in which each security has a significantly different maturity date) portofolio full of bonds with different maturities.

The laddered portofolio has the principal being returned at specific intervals.

When one bond matures, the investor has the chance to reinvest the earnings at the longer-term end if the ladder if he wants to keep it going. If the rates are rising, he has the opportunity to reinvest the maturing principal at higher rates.

Also, if the rates are falling, the portofolio is still earning higher interest on the longer-term holdings.

Another strategy that will help investors manage the interest rate risk is the barbell strategy which means to invest only in short-term and long-term bonds, not intermediates.

The long-term holding will bring attractive coupon rates (stated interest rate on a fixed income security). The short-term holdings give investor the opportunity to invest the money elsewhere if the bond market falls.

Flattening out the Performance of Stock Investments

The stock market returns are more volatile and changeable than the bond market return. So, combining the potential of them will lead to an overall investment portofolio that generates more stable performance over time.

There is a pattern for the movement of bonds and stocks, but it is not a general rule: they move in different directions. So, the bond market rises when the stock market falls and vice versa.

In this way, the downturn of stocks market can be compensated in losses by the performance of bond investments.

Reasons You Might Sell a Bond Before Maturity

There are moments when investors need to sell a bond before maturity:

- They need to realize a loss for tax purposes. Selling a bond before maturity at a loss is a great strategy to offset the tax impact of investment gains. Bond exchange can help achieve a tax purpose without changing the basic profile of the portofolio.

- They need the principal. The buy-and-hold strategy is the most effective long-term strategy, but sometimes things don't work as we expect them to. If an investor sells a bond before maturity, he can get more or less than he had paid for it. If interest rates have risen since the bond was bought, its value will have declined.

If the interest rates have declined, the value of the bond will have increased.

• They are interested in realizing a capital gain. If rates have declined and a bond has appreciated in value, the investor has the opportunity to sell the bond and take the gain rather than continue with the interest. This decision has to be analyzed carefully because the transaction' earnings have to be reinvested at lower interest rates.

• They have accomplished their return objectives. For many investors, the decision of investing in bonds is made with the purpose of getting the total return or income plus capital appreciation or growth. The capital appreciation is achieved when investors sell their investment for more than the purchase's price, when the market offers this opportunity.

Total Return

The strategy of using bonds to invest in total return or a combination of capital appreciation and income can be achieved by using a more active trading plan and having a basis perspective of economy and interest rates.

Total return investors buy bonds when their price is low and sell them when the price has risen, rather than keeping them until maturity.

Bond prices fall when the interest rates are rising. This usually happens when the economy is experiencing an increase.

Some bond funds have total return as the investment objective, providing investors the opportunity to take advantage of bond market movements while leaving the day-to-day investment decisions to professional portofolio managers.

Tax Advantaged Investing

Every investor who is in a high tax bracket may decide to reduce his taxable interest income, keeping more of what he earns.

The interest of U. S. government securities is taxable at the federal level but at the state and the local level they exempt, creating the perfect environment for investments for people who live in high tax states.

The municipal securities offer interest that is exempt from federal income tax and in some cases state and local tax too.

Ladders and barbells can be implemented with municipal securities for a tax-advantaged approach, most accomplished outside of a qualified, tax-deferred retirement or college savings account.

Another way to achieve a tax-related goal for investors is the bond swapping. It is used when the bond has declined in value since purchase but have taxable capital gain from other investment.

Diversifying Risk by Investing in Bond Funds

Investing in bond mutual funds, unit investment trusts or exchange-traded funds are the ideal types of investments for the investors who are interested in achieving automatic diversification of their bond investments for less than it would cost to create a portofolio of individual bonds.

These choices have specific investment objectives and characteristics to match individual needs.

Trading on Market Signals

Have you ever wondered how successful investors managed to translate the market signals into successful trades? Well, knowledge is always the answer.

There are seven bonds market signals in four market-driving categories.

Category: Fundamentals

There are two fundamental forces that drive the bond yields: the inflation and growth.

As an investor, if you understand that bond prices are present values of future cash flows, then you know that forecasts of future growth and inflation are more important than historical data reports of what has already occurred.

Signal one: the market consensus for year-ahead GDP growth.

Signal two: the market consensus for year-ahead inflation.

Trade: a successful investment in this case is to buy a 10-year Treasury note when the consensus lowers its estimate of year-ahead growth and inflation. This means that the interest rates will go down and the bond prices will go up.

The perfect moment to sell the 10-years Treasury note is when the consensus raises its estimate of year-ahead growth and inflation. This means that the interest rates will rise and the prices of the bonds will fall.

Category: Value

This category is based on the presumption that asset prices fluctuate around a steady, long-term equilibrium, extreme deviations help as lead indicators of trend reversals.

The third signal: the real (inflation adjusted) yields

Trade: a successful investment is to buy the 10-year Treasury note when real yields are more than one standard deviation above the long-term moving average sell when they are more than one standard deviation below.

Keep the position until real yields cross the opposite threshold.

Signal four: the ration of the S&P 500 (the American stock market index based on the market capitalization of 500 large companies having common stock listed on the NYSE-New York Stock Exchange and NASDAQ-National Association of Securities Dealers Automated Quotations) earnings yield to the 30-year Treasury yield

Trade: buy bonds when the ratio is more than half a standard deviation below its long-run moving average (this means than bonds are cheap compared to stocks) and sell when it is more than half a standard deviation above its long-term moving average (this happens when the stocks are cheap compared to bonds).

Category: Risk Appetite

The risk appetite is actually the investors' relative preference for safe and risky assets, determined by business cycle fluctuations, policy developments or unexpected events.

Signal five: the JP Morgan Credit Appetite Index, where zero represents the minimum appetite (widest spreads, positive for U. S. government bonds) and 100 represent the maximum appetite (tightest spreads, negative for U. S. government bonds).

Trade: it is the perfect time to sell the U. S. government bonds when credit appetite is high and buy them with it is low.

Category: Technicals

The technical indicators are followers of the market patterns in price and volume.

Signal six: price data.

Trade: you should buy bonds when the short-term moving average of prices traverses the long-term average form below and sell them when it crosses from above.

Signal seven: the flow data. It is defined as the new purchases of U. S. bond market mutual funds, as an indicator of cash flow into the bond market.

Trade: the appropriate moment to buy bonds is when the flow indicator is more than one standard deviation above the long-term moving average and sell them when it is more than one standard deviation below.

The standard deviation is the most oft-used measure of risk when comparing investments.

What does it mean?

An investment with a standard deviation of, say, 3 will give you a return that is within one standard deviation (in this case, 3 percentage points) of the mean about two-thirds of the time. So suppose you have a bond fund that has an historical average annual return of 6 percent, and you know that the standard deviation is 3.

What that means is that two-thirds of the time, the return from this bond fund will fall somewhere between 9 percent (6 percent average return + 3 percent standard deviation) and 3 percent (6 percent average return − 3 percent standard deviation). If that same bond fund had a standard deviation of 5, the returns you could expect would generally fall between 11 percent and 1 percent.

The Morningstar Principia software provides information about the ten-year standard deviation for any bond fund.

It measures how volatile the funds have been for the past ten years.

The higher the number, the greater the price swings in years past and the greater the price swings, most likely, in years to come.